ALL YOU NEED TO KNOW™ ABOUT ETHICS AND FINANCE

2007/8

John Plender
and Avinash D. Persaud

" The subject of business ethics has for too long been relegated to dusty academia or faceless compliance departments. But just as climate change is awakening a new generation to action so the recent corporate hurricanes of Enron and others, have brought business ethics to centre stage. The scandals of the past five years have destroyed lives and resulted in catastrophic financial loss. The message from these is clear – business ignores ethical practices at its peril.

This book is the first of its kind, as its distinguished authors have sought to eschew esoteric discussion for a practical and readable guide for the modern financial or business professional. Plender and Persaud have unique careers that entwine journalism, academia and hands-on business and financial expertise.

Using case studies and an innovative "questions to ask yourself" at the end of each chapter, this is a book that should restore ethical decision making to the front of the minds that run business today.

John Plender has been a senior editorial writer and
columnist at the *Financial Times* since 1981, which he combined until
recently with current affairs broadcasting for the BBC and Channel 4.

After graduating from Oxford University he joined Deloitte, Plender,
Griffiths & Co in1967, qualifying as a chartered accountant in 1970.
He then became financial editor of *The Economist* in 1974, where he
remained until joining the British Foreign Office policy planning staff in
1980. He is a past chairman of Pensions and Investment Research
Consultants (PIRC).

He currently serves as non-executive director of Quintain PLC, a FTSE
250 company, and chairs the advisory council of the Centre For The
Study Of Financial Innovation, a London and New York-based think
tank.

Previous books include *Going Off the Rails – Global Capital and the
Crisis of Legitimacy* (2003); *A Stake in the Future* (1997); *The Square
Mile with Paul Wallace* (1984); and *That's the Way the Money Goes*
(1982).

John Plender was the winner of the Wincott Foundation senior prize for
excellence in financial journalism in 1994.

Avinash D. Persaud's career spans finance,
academia and public policy. He is currently president of Intelligence
Capital Limited, a financial advisory boutique. Previously he was
investment director of GAM London Limited; managing director of
State Street Bank & Trust; global head of Currency and Commodity
Research, J. P. Morgan and director, Debt Research, Union Bank of
Switzerland. He was elected a trustee of the Global Association of
Risk Professionals. Between 1989 and 1999, Persaud was ranked in
the top three of currency analysts for the major institutional investor
surveys.

He is the only person to have won both major awards in international
finance: the Jacques de Larosière (First, 2000) from the Institute of
International Finance, Washington and the Amex Bank Award (Bronze,
1994).

Persaud is Fellow and previously held the Mercer Memorial Chair in
Commerce at Gresham College. He is Visiting Fellow at the
Cambridge Endowment for Research in Finance at the Judge Institute,
Cambridge, and Member of Council, Royal Economics Society.

**Anyone with comments or questions about this book should feel
free to contact the authors at ethics@longtail.eu**

> # WARNING
>
> This book is a concise guide to a complex, multifaceted subject. Given the need to simplify an inherently complex subject, this book is not comprehensive or definitive. Readers must not rely on this book except as a general, schematic overview. Accordingly neither the authors, the publisher, their agents, consultants nor employees accept any liability for any loss (direct or indirect; immediate or consequential; contractual or tortious) however caused from use of this book or reliance upon it.

First published by Longtail Publishing Limited, London, United Kingdom 2007

Tel: 020 7938 1975 Fax: 020 7938 3861 Email: info@longtail.eu

Publisher:	James Piesse
Editorial Assistants:	Leah Bloomberg, Samuel Toombs
Sub-Editor:	Monica Kendall
Typesetting:	Louise Downer
Art Director:	Andrew Debens

ISBN 0-9552186-2-4

ISBN 978-0-9552186-2-0

Printed by: CPI Bath Press

CONTENTS

PREFACE

Writing a book about business ethics inevitably leaves the authors vulnerable to criticism on two main scores. Either they risk being accused of moral superiority, or they leave themselves open to the charge of hypocrisy if they fail to practise what they preach. We should therefore state plainly at the outset that we make no claim to high moral authority in what follows. Nor do we assume we are any less prone to err than others who work in business or who comment on it. Our readiness to plunge into this minefield is simply prompted by a profound conviction that markets work better and companies perform more effectively when they operate within a sound ethical framework.

The idea for the book came originally from Rich Apostolik, chief executive officer of the Global Association of Risk Professionals, of which Avinash is a trustee. As Rich pointed out, finance professionals are routinely required, in various certifications and regulations, to swear by their integrity and good ethics; but no one bothers to explain to them what that actually means. Why not, he asked, write a practical book, not a philosophical treatise, that would help professionals in business and finance make ethically well-considered decisions?

It was also apparent to us that much of the existing literature on business ethics pre-dated the spate of corporate scandals that began with Enron. Part of our purpose has been to explain why those scandals took place despite the growth of a business ethics industry in academia and consultancy, and despite the proliferation across the world of legislation and regulation designed to prevent such scandals happening.

There is a fundamental point to be made here about business risk. The biggest risks most businesses face today stem from human error; and human error often turns on decisions that may appear legal, but which entail ethical abuses that can lead to heavy fines, loss of reputation and a backlash of new, burdensome regulations that impose costs on well-run, ethically sound businesses as well as more dubious enterprises. Ignoring the ethical dimension leaves a gaping hole in any company's risk management.

At the heart of the book is the idea that too many professionals try in some manner to outsource ethical decisions to their compliance officers, lawyers or even competitors. Faced with an ethically challenging transaction they ask, what do the in-house lawyers think and are others doing it? This is not an adequate way to go about the job. We do not claim, though, to have all the right questions and answers. Our aim is simply to try to offer some better questions and to do so in a readable and lively way, using case studies from the real world by way of illustration.

We are grateful to the many professionals who have given us their time to help improve the ideas in this book. Among those to whom we owe a particular debt are Rich Apostolik, Sir Adrian Cadbury, Marion Bell, Ira Millstein, Brandon Davies, Anne Simpson, Daniel Hodson, Philippa Foster Back, Robert A.G. Monks, John Nugee, Michael Stewart, Professor Bishnodat Persaud, Guy Dehn, Betty Barone and Alison Thomas. We are also grateful to Gresham College, which provided welcome research support while Avinash held the Mercer Memorial Chair in Commerce there. Any errors and omissions are, of course, ours alone.

PART 1: Finding the Moral Compass

Chapter 1

WHY THE BUSINESS ETHICS MOVEMENT FAILED

SPEED-READ SUMMARY

- The new millennium has been marked by a succession of corporate scandals prompted by ethical lapses. What started with Enron turned out to be a global phenomenon.

- There are many explanations for this, but the most fundamental concern changes in the structure of incentives in the capital markets. More people are being rewarded in the form of leveraged equity and there is growing pressure on executives to "hit the numbers", which is why some cooked the books.

- Restoring a genuine ethical culture in business, as opposed to one based on compliance, is difficult but necessary because ethics foster trust in business relations. This reduces compliance costs within companies, where ethics operate as a kind of informal internal control, and reduces transaction costs across the wider economy, because high trust reduces the need to resort to costly litigation.

- Ethical lapses have a high cost in the shape of corporate failures and the increased burden of regulation imposed on the economy by lawmakers in response to such failures.

- The purpose of this book is to encourage people to think for themselves and ask questions to arrive at their own judgement about what constitutes "doing the right thing" in the multitude of complex situations thrown up by modern business and finance.

The subject of business ethics has spawned a global growth industry. Together with the related subjects of corporate responsibility and socially responsible investment, it features squarely on the agenda of universities and business schools. Academics have generated a burgeoning literature for those who attend their courses. Companies have embraced the concept of corporate citizenship and published ethical codes they expect managers and employees to follow. Regulators enjoin those they regulate to behave ethically in accordance with publicly disclosed codes. There is just one problem. All this activity has failed to do much good.

Since the turn of the millennium the world has been plagued by a series of corporate scandals that began with Enron, the Texas energy company that collapsed after spectacularly misleading everyone about the true state of its finances. This was far from being a single rotten apple in the barrel of American capitalism. There were scandals at WorldCom, Tyco International, Qwest Communications, Global Crossing, Adelphia, HealthSouth, American International Group, Fannie Mae and sundry others. Europe, too, had its fair share of corporate wrongdoing. The Italian dairy group Parmalat turned out to have perpetrated various frauds and concealed its dire financial position from investors. Royal Dutch Shell, at one time regarded as a beacon of ethical solidity, apparently cooked the books by inflating its production reserves. Another Dutch company, the retail food group Ahold, produced accounts that turned out to be seriously flawed. Volkswagen, the German vehicle maker, was beset by charges of bribery and corruption. In Asia banking crises in Japan, Korea and elsewhere were accompanied by accounting scandals. The causes may have varied from country to country, but a common theme was that the books had been cooked in one way or another.

Of course most companies were not party to such egregious behaviour. Yet the scandals have been sufficiently pervasive to suggest that something has gone wrong with the moral climate in business. Early in 2005 a group of leading US businessmen led by the investment banker Felix Rohatyn, corporate lawyer Martin Lipton and the then New York Stock Exchange chairman John Reed detected what they described as "a disturbing breakdown of values in corporate America". Meeting under the auspices of the American Academy of Arts & Sciences they proposed a new code of ethics containing the business equivalent of the doctors' Hippocratic oath to help restore trust in business. In Europe Hans Blommestein, senior financial economist and head of the capital market programme at the Organisation for Economic Cooperation and Development, the developed world's top official think tank, has even referred to a lowering of ethical standards amounting to a paradigm shift in the business landscape.[1]

A further indication of a flawed ethical climate in the first decade of the new millennium was the way boardroom pay on both sides of the Atlantic soared to unprecedented levels that often bore no relation to corporate performance. And then there was Wall Street, which came in for especially heavy criticism. Investigations by the New York State Attorney General Eliot Spitzer revealed systematic abuse of conflicts of interest in investment banking. Research analysts, who were often paid from the budget of the banks' corporate finance departments, were shown to have cynically puffed technology stocks they knew to be duds. This helped inflate the banks' income from initial public offerings (IPOs), with beneficial consequences for the analysts' own bonuses. Allocations of stock in IPOs during the bull market of the 1990s turned out to have been awarded selectively to favoured clients such as chief executive officers of companies with which the investment banks hoped to do business.

Then came scandals at US mutual funds, which turned out to have been profiting at their investors' expense. Throughout this period of corporate and financial scandals Europe and Japan saw revelations of mis-selling – the financial community's euphemism for ripping off customers – in retail financial services. Perhaps most disturbing of all, the gatekeepers of the public trust in financial markets – accounting firms, lawyers, stock exchanges and rating agencies – were accused of serious failures. Their vital function is to vouch for the integrity and quality of information that is crucial for the efficient working of the markets. The greatest failure was on the part of the auditors, ultimate guarantors of the soundness of the data on which the capitalist system depends, who fell down on the job all across the world, with fatal consequences in the case of Andersen, one of the Big Five accountancy firms.

Alan Greenspan, chairman of the US Federal Reserve, found a phrase that aptly characterised the era: infectious greed. This immediately takes us back to the paradox with which we started, namely that these ethical lapses and violations of the law took place not only at a time when ethical values were much trumpeted by business but also when company law had never been more comprehensive, securities legislation had never been more stringent and corporate governance codes had sprung up here, there and almost everywhere across the globe. So why did the law, regulation and the business ethics movement prove so ineffectual in raising business's ethical game? And what are we to do?

WHAT WENT WRONG

Some argue that bad behaviour was inevitable in the light of the phenomenal stock market bubble of the 1990s. History tells us that when speculation is rife and markets succumb to euphoria, ethical standards do indeed decline as they did in the Dutch tulip mania in the 17th century, the South Sea and Mississippi bubbles in the 18th century and the railroad boom in the 19th century. Others argue that business ethics and corporate responsibility were never more than a cynical public relations ploy, as full of hot air as the stock market bubble. While there is truth in both these assertions we believe that more fundamental factors explain the plethora of scandals and ethical lapses.

The problem starts with the sheer complexity of modern business and finance. To take an obvious example, throughout history people have argued about the morality of usurious interest rates and whether it is appropriate for banks to take deposits from tainted sources. Yet today money has increasingly deserted the banking system for products such as mutual funds, personal pensions and other collective savings vehicles which give rise to a plethora of more complex conflicts of interest than exist in deposit taking and lending. Financial products, moreover, are increasingly difficult to understand, especially in the new derivatives markets where financial institutions trade in instruments such as swaps, futures and options. Much of this trade takes place not on open, transparent exchanges but between individual institutions. And a large proportion of this trade does not appear on the face of the institutions' balance sheets. This is important because transparency is a key support for ethical behaviour. And a lack of transparency makes a business difficult to regulate. These new markets thus pose exceptionally difficult challenges for lawmakers, regulators and gatekeepers such as auditors and rating agencies, who find it hard to keep up with rapid financial innovation.

The problem of complexity is compounded by the legislative and regulatory response to corporate and banking scandals. The greater the number of laws, rules and regulations, the more people are tempted to stop thinking about the ethical consequences of their actions and to focus more narrowly on compliance. A mentality sets in whereby ticking the box is regarded as satisfying all ethical as well as regulatory requirements. It is worth noting that the growth of ethical codes in the US was partly aimed at reducing corporate exposure to punitive damages in negligence claims. Under sentencing law and guidelines, fines on companies can be substantially reduced if they can show they have effective programmes to prevent and detect violations of law. So for many companies business ethics amounted to no more than an opportunistic device to reduce the penalties for unethical behaviour. The overall danger here is captured by the French adage *trop de loi tue la loi* – too much law kills the law. The extraordinarily legalistic culture in the US, in particular, gives people a strong motivation to shuffle off responsibility to others and to cover their back.

Technology, too, has played a part, in that the number of financial transactions taking place without personal contact has increased exponentially. That ought to mean that more trust and more ethical behaviour are necessary to make markets work efficiently and keep transaction costs low. In practice it has not always worked like that. New techniques such as credit scoring distance bankers from individual customers: money is lent on something not unlike a scattergun principle, the underlying assumption being that a given percentage will default and that the percentage represents an acceptable business risk. Such techniques often ignore the fiduciary concept which requires bankers to "know their customer". In the English-speaking countries where credit tends to be extended more readily than in continental Europe and parts of Asia people are showered with unsolicited offers of credit without any rigorous assessment of their financial circumstances and current levels of indebtedness. In the extreme (but common) case, credit line increases on credit and store cards are made on an automatic and unsolicited basis so long as a minimum payment is being made on the card. Undoubtedly the liberalisation of credit markets has increased freedom and choice. Yet it has also brought ethically questionable banking practices that contribute to a growing problem of over-indebtedness, which may soon rank on a par with alcoholism in terms of the social damage it does.

The sheer pace of corporate change has posed a huge challenge, too, to the ethical climate. Thirty years ago corporate life was relatively staid and the opportunities for individual advancement were much less. Today there are great opportunities for everyone in an increasingly meritocratic culture. More is at stake for individuals at all levels of the firm, which means that their ethical dilemmas are more acute. And the development of a market in corporate control – takeover and merger activity in plain English – spurs constant changes of management and corporate upheavals, especially in the anglophone world. Such changes are often followed by ethical breakdowns because there can be great uncertainty in the company about the values of an enlarged or shrunken organisation. If business leaders fail to convey a clear and swift message as to how they expect people to behave and to do the right thing at a time of radical corporate upheaval, an ethical culture can rapidly be eroded. In an old but useful phrase, "the tone at the top", in such circumstances, is crucial.

Business schools must bear some responsibility for ethical failures in the corporate sector. The two main architects of the debacle at Enron, Jeffrey Skilling and Andy Fastow, had MBAs from top US business schools, respectively Harvard and Northwestern. In many of the other scandals, finance professionals who cooked the books were also graduates of leading business schools. Part of the trouble is that many schools have put business ethics in a ghetto, treating it as a discrete business subject requiring a course of its own. Far better, says Ira Millstein, governance pioneer and director of the Yale School of Management's Center for Corporate Governance and Performance, to embed business ethics in other courses. If you do a course in marketing or finance, you should, he argues, be invited to consider the kinds of ethical dilemmas that you will face in the real world and discuss how comfortable you are with the different possible responses. This is surely preferable to turning business ethics into an academic discipline of its own.

There are some who suggest, too, that business schools have been stuck in an ivory tower and measure themselves not by their understanding of important drivers of business performance but by the rigour of their scientific research. In the attempt to turn business studies into a science, it is suggested, business academics have emptied their theories of ethical content.[2]

A further critique is that the assumptions of economics and of modern finance theory in which these people were grounded operated as a malign substitute for an ethical framework. Finance theory puts heavy emphasis on the behaviour of "rational" agents who seek to maximise their own welfare through opportunistic behaviour. The pursuit of material wealth is assumed to be the justification for individual and group behaviour. For anyone lacking much of a moral conscience this amounts to an implicit ethical – or rather, unethical – agenda, given that acting other than opportunistically is perceived as irrational.

This view of individuals as personal utility maximisers is a narrow version of the creed of mainstream economists since Adam Smith, who believe that allowing individuals to pursue their self-interest through the market achieves the greatest good for society. Smith was also an early proponent of agency theory – the belief that agents who act for a principal will never do as good a job as they would do if they were performing the same task for themselves. Yet Adam Smith was not only the author of *The Wealth of Nations* but of *The Theory of Moral Sentiments*. It would not have occurred to him that the pursuit of economic self-interest should take place outside a moral context or that it would be good even if pursued at the cost of doing serious harm to others. The modern, one-dimensional view of Adam Smith's work incorporates a remarkably narrow implicit view of human motivation. The narrowness is particularly apparent in approaches to corporate governance based on the more extreme versions of agency theory. In implying that managers cannot be trusted to do their jobs, there is a risk that managers who feel they are not trusted will become less trustworthy.

It is worth emphasising here that what happens in the early days of an employee's career tends to have an enduring influence on his or her attitude to morality in business. Equipped with a finance theory mindset and projected into an organisation where the culture is one whose focus is exclusively about delivering on targets or winning new business no matter what, an employee is being powerfully steered towards self-seeking opportunism rather than "doing the right thing".

Unfortunately, the burgeoning ethics industry has often implicitly encouraged such attitudes by arguing that business ethics and corporate responsibility are profitable because they enhance corporate reputation. Yet anyone who believes that honesty is the best policy because it is profitable is clearly not honest. Dealing with such a person carries the risk that they may change their mind and decide that there is more profit in dishonesty. That said, a bad apple may be immune to education and environment anyway. Enron's Jeffrey Skilling started his career at McKinsey at a time when this famous management consultancy was widely admired for its high ethical standards. Those standards clearly failed to rub off on him.

PRESSURE TO HIT THE NUMBERS

Perhaps the most fundamental deterioration in the ethical climate in business arose as a by-product of the seismic shift in corporate governance that took place in the economies of the English-speaking countries in the late 1980s and early 1990s. An era in which managers enjoyed paternalistic power with relatively little accountability gave way to one in which greater emphasis was placed on shareholder value. Over the course of the last decade of the 20th century, pressure on chief executive officers from the capital markets increased exponentially. Fund managers, analysts and the media have become vocal in their demands for value.

The requirement for quarterly reporting bred a "hitting the numbers" culture. Chief executives who failed to meet the market's expectations could find themselves in the ejector seat as the share price collapsed. In the English-speaking countries the CEO's average tenure came down to as little as three or four years. With top jobs on the line there was thus a huge increase in the temptation to cook the books – especially given the short time period accorded to chief executives to establish credibility with markets. The cooking could be done legally, whether through juggling with accounting principles with the approval of auditors or changing the timing of spending decisions. Or it could be done illegally as at WorldCom where the accounting fiddle was a multi-billion dollar fraud. Or, again, a chief executive could make an ambitious takeover, which envelops corporate performance in a temporary accounting fog. Or health and safety standards could be sacrificed in the interests of short-term profitability, as is alleged to have happened at the oil giant BP.

A second radical change in the 1990s was the growing adoption of performance-related or equity-type incentives, whether in the form of conventional bonuses or stock option awards. Stock options were justified on the grounds that they aligned managers' interests with those of shareholders, thereby overcoming the agency problem identified by Adam Smith. Here the temptation came from the carrot – a desire to enhance personal rewards – rather than the stick. But it tended towards a similar outcome: more cooking of the books to engineer bigger bonuses or increases in the share price to enhance the value of stock options. Taken together, capital market discipline and stock option awards have had a very powerful impact on motivation. So, too, did the stock market bubble. As with earlier bubbles a euphoric rise in share prices put moral values to the test. At each new and higher level of the market, all those who were paid in the form of stock options or shares faced an added temptation to cut corners in pursuit of a fast stock market buck. The potential rewards for bad behaviour kept increasing as the market went up. It is sometimes rather crudely said that everyone has their price. While this may not be universally true, it is certainly the case that a stock market bubble acts as a moral price discovery process, but with the twist that the 1990s' bubble was unique not just in size but in scope because more people were being rewarded in equity than ever before.

The existence of individual pension plans for employees as well as stock option and other equity incentive schemes for executives turned the moral price discovery process into a widespread national phenomenon in the US and to a lesser extent elsewhere. When people at the top tried to push up the company's share price by cooking the books, more people down below became complicit in the scam. They were heavily incentivised not to blow the whistle. The globalisation of capital also meant that the technology bubble was transmitted across the world. Asian and continental European companies that had hitherto paid employees according to seniority started tentatively to reward people with equity.

A third radical change concerned the transformation of the business model of professions such as accountancy and the law. Until recently the professions operated as self-regulatory cartels. Competition was limited and partners were rewarded on the basis of seniority rather than performance. In the 1980s things changed as the professions joined in the general move towards a more individualistic, free market orientation. Partners were increasingly paid according to what business they brought in: an "eat what you kill" culture. The big accountancy firms turned themselves into multi-service conglomerates, expanding out of the core audit business into more glamorous consultancy. Audit, with its limited scope for rapid growth, became a poor relation within fast-expanding businesses where the professional ethos went into inexorable decline.

The world is now moving closer to the US model of capitalism and to a business culture in which equity plays an increasingly vital part. So while much of what happened during the bubble could be regarded as an extreme response to highly exceptional circumstances, it is important to recognise that the incentives and penalties that produced that misconduct not only remain in place, but are having a wider geographical impact. A pervasive theme of the narrative and case studies of this book will be the vital and absolute importance of ensuring that incentive structures both within the organisation and in the capital markets push people in a direction that is not at odds with ethical behaviour. We suspect that the failure of the Sarbanes-Oxley Act and the various post-Enron regulatory initiatives around the world to confront this vital issue of incentives – except by the crude expedient of imposing greater penalties for bad behaviour – means that a greater burden may be placed on business ethics in future than it is capable of bearing.

A TIME FOR REALISM

In the light of this rather downbeat verdict it is worth asking whether expectations of business ethics should be sharply downgraded. Does realism dictate that we leave it to the bishops to wring their hands over recent events while paying closer attention to the sermons of free market economists such as Milton Friedman? It was Friedman who said that "few trends could so thoroughly undermine the very foundations of our free society as the acceptance by corporate officials of a social responsibility other than to make as much money for their stockholders as possible". Corporations, unlike individuals, could not have a moral responsibility for their actions, he argued, and the limit of management's obligations beyond maximising profits was compliance with the law.[3] Or should realism be taken to the extremes considered by Albert Carr in a seminal article in the *Harvard Business Review* entitled: "Is Business Bluffing Ethical"?[4] He argued that business could not be expected to adhere to the moral standards adopted by society at large but should be seen in the same light as a poker game where setting out deliberately to deceive and to lie is acceptable behaviour. This cleverly translates Machiavelli's argument that it may be necessary to do wrong in the interests of the state into a business context.

We believe that the time has indeed come for more realism about business ethics and corporate responsibility, though not in the way these arguments imply. For the assumption underlying the Friedmanite position is one of perfect competition, perfectly responsible governments and sound laws. Yet companies often affect society in ways that are not adequately regulated by the market or by laws and state regulations. Corporate activity can, for example, generate side effects known as externalities. When this happens, market prices fail to reflect true social costs and benefits so that the natural alignment between profit maximisation and social welfare ceases to work. Some argue that it is the job of elected politicians to legislate for externalities. But there is no system of global governance capable of addressing issues such as loss of biodiversity, global warming or cross-border externalities. The law catches up with developments in markets only with a lag and the shortness of the electoral cycle makes it difficult for governments to cope with long-term issues. Indeed, governments are often part of the problem rather than the solution. And the minimalist Friedmanite formula is certainly inadequate in the context of developing countries, where enforcement of the law is often deficient. Unethical behaviour – self-interested behaviour that inflicts harm on others – can be very profitably pursued in many developing countries at high cost to their populations without any legal penalty being imposed on the perpetrator.

Even in the developed world the law may codify a basic level of morality where there is a strong consensus, but the lowest common denominator will not cover the countless grey areas where business people have to make difficult judgements. There are even times when laws do not just act too mildly in favour of someone's morality, but they act against morality. The pre-civil rights period in the United States, Germany in the 1940s and Myanmar today offer cases in point.

RESTATING THE CASE FOR BUSINESS ETHICS

Exclusive reliance on the law, then, is not enough. There is a role for business ethics and corporate responsibility, even if some of their advocates have made exaggerated claims for what they can do, for example, to alleviate global poverty. And it is worth pointing out that companies can maintain or increase profits through corporate responsibility when this helps them anticipate and pre-empt costly future regulations. In a world where an increasing number of customers has an ethical agenda and those customers are willing to pay more for goods produced to social and environmental standards that go beyond what is required by law, companies can profitably respond to this demand or, on the negative side, avoid consumer boycotts by eschewing what their customers regard as ethically questionable behaviour.

As for Friedman's views on corporate conscience, we prefer the formulation of an earlier American sage, Henry David Thoreau, who remarked: "It is true enough said that a corporation has not conscience. But a corporation of conscientious men is a corporation with a conscience." In other words, when we refer to a company's values or standards we are saying no more than that the people in the company are responsible for its actions and their decisions collectively establish the company's values. It should also be said that Milton Friedman qualified his minimalist assertion about maximising profits by referring to the need to do so "within the rules of the game", which he defined as "the basic rules of the society, both those embodied in law and those embodied in ethical custom". He also counselled against resort to deception in business.

That more nuanced approach accords more closely with the reality that business operates in the social system and its activities have social consequences. And in the running of a business most decisions cannot be taken on the basis of a pure economic calculus. It makes practical sense to recognise that ethics provide a complement to the internal constitution (or memorandum and articles) of the company which sets out the objects and rules for the conduct of the company's business. Likewise, that the contract between management and shareholders is necessarily incomplete: shareholders cannot be expected to sanction each and every decision taken by operational management. In fact most shareholders – and not just ethical investment funds – would wish management to avoid making the maximum possible profit if, to take the most obvious case, this entailed abuses of human rights. How many pension scheme beneficiaries would be happy to profit from the building of a pipeline in Myanmar with forced labour? There are occasions when management has to make its best judgement of shareholders' views and allow ethics to trump a narrow profit-maximising course of action.[5]

In practice a majority of managers in the developed world do take that view. A survey by consultants McKinsey, published in 2006, found that the global business community had embraced the idea that it should play a wider role in society. More than four out of five respondents agreed that generating higher returns for investors should be accompanied by broader contributions to the public good – for example, providing good jobs, making philanthropic donations and going beyond legal requirements to minimise pollution and other negative effects of business. Only one in six agreed with the idea that high returns should be a corporation's sole focus.[6] Increasingly companies see corporate responsibility as a form of risk management. The more sophisticated use options theory to establish how much to invest in specific corporate responsibility projects as a means of reducing earnings and share price volatility.[7]

THE IMPORTANCE OF TRUST

The argument of this book is that the discipline of business ethics, defined at its simplest as examining what is right or wrong in a business context, is far from being a lost cause and ought to be a matter of continuing high priority. Expressed in broad terms the reason is not just that the law is inadequate but that ethics are vitally important in business and finance because of the role of trust in business relations. That is the rejoinder to Albert Carr. Trust creates social capital which facilitates cooperative behaviour both in society and in organisations. Bad behaviour erodes trust and forces people to place heavier reliance on the law and on regulation. And the more transactions have to be governed by contract, the more cumbersome and expensive business becomes, as everything has to be negotiated, agreed, litigated and enforced. Such legalism, when it is a substitute for trust, gives rise to what economists call transaction costs. As the American thinker Francis Fukuyama has argued, a lack of trust at the societal level imposes a kind of tax on all forms of economic activity.[8] At the level of the company ethics are an informal, low-cost substitute for internal control within the company and for external regulation without. High ethical standards in a company mean that less expenditure on internal controls, audit systems and auditors is needed to prevent fraud and other chicanery.

The point can be seen at its most basic in relation to the public corporation. The corporate form has proved itself over centuries to be the most flexible and durable vehicle for wealth creation. It deals with other people's money and those people would not be willing to advance their money to the corporation without some trust and protection. It is, of course, possible to run an organisation efficiently without trust and without integrity. Colombian drug syndicates do this. But it requires punitive management and control, without which these organisations would fall apart. Where there is a deficiency of ethical values and an absence of trust in more conventional business it is similarly necessary to fall back on punitive laws and regulations, though of a less violent kind. The draconian Sarbanes-Oxley Act in the US is a pre-eminent example.

What this means in practical business terms has been well expressed by the late Marvin Bower, the inspirational leader who turned McKinsey into the most respected and widely admired of consultancy firms. He noted that executives in well-run companies often referred to "our philosophy" or "the way we do things round here" – a simple but subtle phrase that can contain a moral dimension without sounding sanctimonious. Such a philosophy evolves as a set of rules or guidelines that gradually become established, through trial and error or through leadership, as expected patterns of behaviour. Within that philosophy, Bower argued, the maintenance of high ethical standards was essential to maximum success because ethical businesses had three primary advantages over competitors with lower standards, namely:

- A business of high principle generates greater drive and effectiveness because people know that they can do the *right* thing decisively and with confidence. When there is any doubt about what action to take, they can rely on the guidance of ethical principles. Inner administrative drive emanates largely from the fact that everyone feels confident that they can safely do the right thing immediately. And they also know that any action that is even slightly unprincipled will be generally condemned.
- A business of high principle attracts high-calibre people more easily, thereby gaining a basic competitive and profit edge. A high-calibre person favours the business of principle and avoids

15

the employer whose practices are questionable. For this reason, companies that do not adhere to high ethical standards must actually maintain a higher level of compensation to attract and hold people of ability.

■ A business of high principle develops better and more profitable relations with customers, competitors and the general public because it can be counted on to do the right thing at all times. By the consistently ethical character of its actions, it builds a favourable image. In choosing among suppliers, customers resolve their doubts in favour of such a company. Competitors are less likely to comment unfavourably on it. And the general public is more likely to be open-minded towards its actions.[9]

Bower's views may not have held good in the aberrant period of the 1990s stock market bubble. Enron, for example, was clearly able to recruit talented people. But over longer periods of time and under more normal circumstances, we believe his case is persuasive. The benefits to shareholders of ethical behaviour and corporate responsibility can be immediate and tangible. To cite just one example, Southwest Airlines at the turn of the millennium was regarded as one of the most considerate employers in the US airline industry. It was the only US airline not to lay anyone off after the terrorist attack on New York's Twin Towers. The following year the company received 120,000 applicants for 3,000 jobs and it was the only sizeable US airline to make a profit.[10]

There is now an academic literature that lends support to Marvin Bower's point about the connection between moral principle and business success.[11] Yet it is striking how so many companies have tried to impose ethics on their organisation through codes promulgated from on high, by instituting ethical hotlines and appointing ethics officers instead of relying on the evolutionary process of trial and error Bower describes, which is the very opposite of a compliance culture. Note, too, that Bower, with an unrivalled knowledge of the corporate world, is with Thoreau rather than Friedman in choosing to refer to the "ethical character" of the company.

To consider in more detail how trust reduces transaction costs in an economy while lack of trust increases them, take the case of insider dealing, which until recently was not illegal in many countries. Among the victims of insider dealing are market makers, the people at the heart of the stock market who are obliged to carry an inventory of stock. In a market where insider dealers are active, the market makers are forced to widen their bid and offer spreads – the margin between the buying and selling price of the stock – to protect themselves from the consequences of being on the wrong side of a deal where the insider profits at their expense. In other words an extra cushion of profit is needed to cover the cost of being ambushed by insiders and for investors that amounts to an additional dealing cost. At the same time investors will pay less for new issues when companies are floated on the stock market because they have to be compensated for the risk of being exploited by insiders. Academic research has in fact shown that in jurisdictions where insider dealing is effectively policed the cost of equity capital decreases significantly.[12] In extreme cases a lack of trust may even lead to a fundamental undermining of markets. If, for example, a market develops a reputation for being full of rogue traders, then individuals will begin to disengage from it. As the market shrinks, market makers are forced to widen their dealing spreads further. If the phenomenon becomes general across the markets, it ultimately reduces the growth of the economy.

Something like this happened in the UK as a result of mis-selling scandals whereby financial advisers and salespeople introduced clients to investments, pension plans and home loans that were unsuitable for their personal circumstances. The intermediaries applied heavy pressure to people to buy inappropriate products because they were rewarded according to the volume of their sales, not sensitivity to the clients' real needs. Disillusionment among the British public with the abuse of this conflict of interest became so widespread that people began to shun collective savings vehicles, contributing to a crisis of inadequate provision for pensions. Many even took to investing in buy-to-let housing to save for their retirement instead of taking out pension plans.

THE VALUE OF ETHICS IN FINANCE

Trust, on which the economic case for business ethics substantially rests, is particularly important in financial markets. This becomes apparent if we compare finance with retail markets. With food, drink and clothes consumers are quick to detect poor quality and will take their custom elsewhere. In contrast, retail financial decisions are relatively infrequent. Most people make a decision on their pension only when they join the pension scheme and when they are preparing to leave it. By the time you discover you have made a mistake with a pension, mortgage or car loan it may be too late to do much about it. This makes it harder for the financial markets to root out rogues than in other industries. And in practice banks and other financial institutions that engage in widespread mis-selling rarely go out of business. They are usually fined by the regulatory authorities, with the cost often being borne not by the people who did the mis-selling but by the shareholders who were innocent bystanders or even by the customers if they were buying from a mutually owned organisation.

The nub of it is that much of finance is about promises whose fulfilment takes place over time. Those promises need to be sustained by trust, which cannot exist without an ethical framework. Despite this fundamental point there is a high degree of cynicism in parts of the financial system about business ethics. Many employees simply shed their moral sensibilities as they walk through the company doors. It is generally agreed that the ethical tone of an organisation is set at the top and that business leaders need to send a clear message about "the way we do things here". Yet many employers delegate the task of establishing and implementing a corporate values statement to an ethics officer who turns to outside consultants who churn out values statements for all and sundry. Too often, no attempt is then made to embed the values throughout the organisation. In effect, the people at the top outsource ethics. An internal market then develops to shift moral responsibility around the organisation. There is also a growing tendency for top executives to recycle moral responsibility outside the organisation. After the 1990s' bubble many chief financial officers and corporate treasurers who shunted liabilities off the balance sheet into special purpose vehicles, thereby misleading shareholders, were prone to say that it was all the idea of the investment banks. So, too, in the case of ailing Japanese banks that turned to US and European investment banks for derivatives trading strategies that allowed them to window dress stretched balance sheets at the year end.

Even when an organisation realises that there have been ethical failures, as Citigroup, the giant financial services group, did in 2004, efforts to educate employees, especially in a global business, tend to run into problems at the level of the trading floor. In investment banking many traders see themselves as hired guns who rent capital from the bank to pursue profitable short-term trading opportunities that will bump up their bonuses. If an opportunity for bigger bonuses arises at the bank next door such traders quickly decamp. This is profoundly destructive of attempts to create an ethical ethos. For where people lack a sense of loyalty to the organisation it is difficult to embed a set of common values or make them think about the collateral damage their actions may inflict on other stakeholders in the bank such as important clients. Equally problematic is that investment bankers can make multi-millions of dollars on as little as one or two deals. The temptation to cut corners when you know that it will make you rich for life is hard for many to resist.

THE HIGH COST OF THE ETHICAL DEFICIT

For those who remain sceptical about the case for business ethics it is necessary only to point to the high price we all now pay for the ethical lapses and losses of trust in the era of infectious greed. Important innovative companies such as Enron, WorldCom and Parmalat collapsed as a direct result of their managements' ethical shortcomings, taking jobs, employees' pensions and investors' savings with them. After the excesses of recent years there has been a raft of new legislation and new regulations across the world in an attempt to restore public confidence. Yet it is not possible to legislate or regulate people into good behaviour. That much is clear from the fact that scandals have continued to break. If the public is to be persuaded of the legitimacy of wealth creation, trust in business and finance has to be rebuilt and a more robust ethical climate established. The evidence of the opinion polls around the world suggests there is a long way to go.

As we argued earlier, restoring trust, which requires an ethical support system, has the potential to reduce transaction costs in the economy and in individual companies. So the chapters that follow seek to explore the ethical issues that face financiers, managers, regulators and employees today, to look at the kind of questions that can usefully be asked where the law and regulation are silent and to pinpoint a handful of basic ethical principles that should command widespread support as a means of handling difficult dilemmas in an ever more challenging commercial environment. We make no apology for omitting detailed discussion of the different ethical theories. This is intended to be a practical book for people working in areas such as finance, risk management, banking and trading, and in advisory roles, as well as a book about the wider phenomenon of business ethics. For those who want to explore virtue ethics, deontological ethics, teleological ethics and the various other strands of thinking on this subject there are many excellent academic books on the market. Our aim, rather, is to encourage people to think and question in order to come to their own conclusions as to what doing the right thing means when faced with the extraordinary variety of ethical dilemmas thrown up by modern business.

NOTES

1   Public Trust in *Danger, Finance & Common Good*, 18–19 (Spring–Summer 2004).

2   For an extended critique of the business schools' approach, see *Bad Management Theories Are Destroying Good Management Practices*, Academy of Management Learning & Education (2005, Vol. 4, No.1) 75 – 91, by Sumantra Ghoshal of the Advanced Institute of Management Research, UK and London Business School.

3   Milton Friedman, *Capitalism & Freedom* (University of Chicago Press, 1962).

4   Albert Carr, *Harvard Business Review*, 46 (January–February 1968).

5   For the case against corporate social responsibility, see the survey in *The Economist* of 22 January 2005, which takes a more extreme position than Milton Friedman. For the case for and a critique of *The Economist*'s survey, see *The Good Company: Confronting the Main Stream* by Franck Amalric, Head of the Research Center for Corporate Responsibility and Sustainability at the University of Zurich, *Finance & Common Good*, 21 (Spring 2005). We have used the term corporate responsibility throughout since corporate social responsibility has a connotation in the United States of philanthropy.

6   *The McKinsey Quarterly* (2006, No. 2).

7   See *Take My Profits, Please! Volatility Reduction and Ethics*, a lecture by Professor Michael Mainelli to Gresham College in London, March 2006, for specific examples of how companies perform cost-benefit analysis on corporate responsibility investments.

8   Francis Fukuyama, *Trust: The Social Virtues and the Creation of Prosperity* (Hamish Hamilton, 1995).

9   This is an extract from Marvin Bower's *The Will to Manage: Corporate Success through Programmed Management* (McGraw-Hill, 1966).

10 Lots of it About – Corporate Social Responsibility, *The Economist* (14 December 2002.).

11 See, for example, Doug Lennick and Fred Kiel, *Moral Intelligence: Enhancing Business Performance & Leadership Success* (Wharton School Publishing, 2005).

12 See Utpal Bhattacharya and Hazem Daouk, *The World Price of Insider Trading*, *Journal of Finance*: 57: 1 (2002).

Chapter 2

HOW TO DO YOUR OWN ETHICAL THING

SPEED-READ SUMMARY

■ Globalisation poses difficult ethical challenges for companies since implementing a single ethical code in subsidiaries and branches across the world runs into the problem of disparate religious traditions and cultures.

■ Most people, whatever their nationality or religion, believe in fundamental virtues such as truth, freedom and reverence for life. In business, too, there are some absolute values. Bribery and corruption are universally accepted as wrong, although the weight attached to this judgement may vary, as will the definition of bribery and corruption, from country to country.

■ Compliance is no substitute for individuals making their own ethical judgements. We look at three specific ethical dilemmas confronted by an owner-manager, an expatriate middle manager and an investment bank employee.

■ While there are some ethical principles in business that hold good for ever, perceptions of acceptable practice change over time. We illustrate this by looking at a scandal that occurred in the financial crisis that followed the bubble economy period in Japan.

For much of the 20th century most managers and employees confronted ethical dilemmas primarily in a national context. In the 21st century ethical issues are increasingly addressed on a global basis. As well as having foreign subsidiaries and branches, many of the biggest businesses have scores of foreign investors on their share registers. This growth in cross-border direct and portfolio investment raises big questions. Are there absolute values in business ethics that apply regardless of place and time in this era of globalisation? Or are those who work in transnational corporations condemned to deal with relative values that change according to the nations, religions and cultures in the different locations where they do business? Is it a vain hope to aspire to a single ethical code that can usefully be applied by a company, a partnership or a profession all across the world?

Perceptions about business ethics are undoubtedly heavily influenced by local values, history and cultures. Confucian values such as respect for tradition, hierarchy and sacrifice influence Asian economies, the structure of companies and the behaviour of individuals across that region. The behaviour of the large networks of Chinese and Indian expatriate businesses in Asia is strongly influenced by the family ownership that is critical to the current structure of most Asian companies. For Japanese salarymen, the company is the family to which they owe their loyalty – a case of the Confucian duty of sacrificing oneself if need be to the state being transferred from the state to the corporation.

In countries with a Confucian tradition beliefs are less important than behaviour and goals. In contrast, the Islamic and Christian traditions emphasise creeds and absolute values as well as practice. In the English-speaking world behaviour is more individualistic. And in many countries there are multiple value systems. This is obviously true of those like the United States which have been peopled by immigrants from countless different backgrounds. But it is equally true of others such as India, which has, among other religions, Jainism, Sikhism, Zoroastrianism and Islam as well as Hinduism.

If that sounds a challenging background against which to address ethical questions it is worth stating that there is nothing new about the challenge, any more than there is about globalisation. When Warren Hastings, the first Governor-General of India, was impeached in the British parliament in 1787 on charges ranging from procuring judicial murder to extortion, part of the argument turned on whether English standards or the lower standards deemed to prevail in India should be used to judge Hastings's behaviour. Edmund Burke, the Whig politician and political philosopher who opened the trial in parliament, was in no doubt that absolute standards should apply. Hastings was, incidentally, in the vanguard of globalisation, having started his career as an employee of the East India Company.

FUNDAMENTAL VIRTUES

We believe that there are more absolute values that apply in business than might seem obvious at first sight. Regardless of where you are in the world, most people believe in fundamental virtues. Extensive survey research done with the Gallup Organization by the Institute for Global Ethics has shown that in all nations values such as truth, compassion, responsibility, freedom, reverence for life and fairness are regarded as hugely important by the great majority of people.[1] Different countries may accord different weights to each of these values. But they are nonetheless common to all. It is hard to believe that the same is not true of values in a business context. Most people, for example, would agree that bribery and corruption are wrong. It is the definition and tolerance of bribery and corruption that varies between countries and cultures, not the ethical yardstick itself. The practical ethical difficulty for managers and employees turns on questions such as what payments can be made to win orders. The distinction between a gift and a bribe is not always clear and the distinction will be differently perceived in different countries. Note, too, that if a company decides not to do business in a country where bribery and corruption are endemic, both company and inhabitants of the country may be disadvantaged.

On human rights, most people would also agree that child labour is bad. But there can be a clash of absolute values. In parts of Asia,

Africa and Latin America, prohibiting child labour could further impoverish desperately poor families. The ethical dilemma for companies partly boils down to deciding which is the lesser of two evils, but managers who oppose the principle of child labour while tolerating it in their subsidiaries in the Third World cannot escape the charge of hypocrisy.

Much of the Universal Declaration of Human Rights would serve as a moral compass for both companies and individuals. But not all of it, especially in its economic prescriptions. The call for equal pay for equal work, for example, would deny the world's poorest countries the one comparative advantage they enjoy in the world economy: the cheapness of their labour. Without cheap labour many of today's most successful economies in Asia would not have reached the point of economic takeoff.

A HANDFUL OF GLOBAL NORMS

It is not an impossible task, then, for companies to incorporate universal norms in their own ethical codes that can be applied anywhere in the world. Here are four potential examples. An obvious starting point is compliance with the law. In most cases flouting the law will be clearly unethical. It cannot be right, for example, for companies to operate a business model where fines for criminal activity in relation to health and safety or treatment of the environment are simply regarded as a normal operating cost of doing business. Where the law is bad, as was the case with the abhorrent racist apartheid laws in South Africa, the ethical dilemma for managers is whether to engage with the problem and try to change the law, or simply to withdraw. A company may even do both. General Motors tried to engage by establishing a set of principles to run its business in South Africa which violated the apartheid laws and insisted that employees should be paid according to merit without regard to race. It eventually concluded that its efforts were doing nothing to undermine apartheid, so it sold its South African subsidiary.

A second universal norm could be to avoid damaging the health and safety of employees and the public. Safety standards are inevitably lower and accident rates higher in developing countries.

Yet this, once again, is a case of greater tolerance of cornercutting behaviour in places where poverty is the norm rather than one of different relative moral values. Only a cynic would argue that a high accident rate constitutes a comparative advantage for an economy and that it was acceptable for companies from advanced economies to take greater risks with their employees in the Third World. What is more, many companies in the developed world appear perfectly able to take the safety standards of their home country to host countries without sustaining a significant loss of competitive advantage.

It is also surely unethical for First World companies operating in the developing world to exploit weak or deficient laws in ways that disadvantage the local population. A notable example has arisen where companies have engaged in practices such as toxic waste dumping to make a profit while jeopardising the lives and health of the local community in very poor countries run by corrupt governments that welcome the dumpers. There will always be entrepreneurs who are willing to take advantage of that situation, just as there will always be government ministers willing to take bribes from them. But the ethics of toxic dumping are usually clear cut. To say that if we do not seize the opportunity, someone else will – an excuse also often used to justify arms sales to vicious regimes – is a moral opt out. Moreover, on environmental issues Western companies have shown that a universal norm is possible. General Electric of the US builds its plants around the world to US Environmental Protection Agency standards or to local standards if they are higher. (They often are, even in the Third World: in Mexico, stipulations on groundwater are much tougher than in the US.) GE says that it has not suffered competitive disadvantage by observing a global minimum standard based on the US.

A third universal norm might be truthful reporting of corporate performance. This may sound like a pious hope when financial figures are routinely massaged by CEOs and CFOs who are keen to boost the value of their stock option and equity share entitlements. But it remains a universal norm even if some people feel it is honoured more in the breach than the observance. And if companies adopt it in a code of values there is a greater chance that the rights and wrongs of creative accounting issues will be discussed rather than swept under the carpet.

A fourth might be to safeguard the interests of minority shareholders. This could appear controversial in parts of continental Europe and Asia where corporate governance operates on the blockholder principle whereby dominant shareholders often use their voting strength to extract private benefits of control at minority shareholders' expense. Certainly attitudes are very different on this score from those prevailing in the English-speaking world. The German banker Carl Furstenberg showed just how different with his famous remark that "shareholders are stupid and impertinent – stupid because they give their money to somebody else without any effective control over what this person is doing with it, and impertinent because they ask for a dividend as a reward for their stupidity". The underlying assumption is that the outside shareholder is a free rider and therefore does not deserve to be looked after. And in one sense the free rider accusation is true. A dominant shareholder or lead bank with effective voting control can often impose better governance and secure better management than dispersed shareholders with uncoordinated voting power. So in blockholder systems outside shareholders are invited to join the game in the knowledge that they may enjoy the benefits of good governance and tight shareholder control – or they may be fleeced. But fleecing shareholders is not right, even if it is common practice in some countries. It is just a sophisticated form of theft. With the growing influence of US and UK investors in capital markets around the world the unfair treatment dished out to minority shareholders may ultimately be seen for what it is: unethical behaviour.

The list could easily be extended – readers are invited to do so for themselves. Note, too, that leading professions accept the case for universal norms. Concepts such as independence or avoiding putting your own interests before those of the client are universally applicable, even if the definition of independence may vary according to the place. And is it beyond the wit of human beings to find a definition of independence that is acceptable globally for ethical and governance purposes? A similar list could readily be put together for employees. Using company resources for personal purposes, taking credit for other people's work or calling in sick in order to enjoy paid leisure time are reprehensible things regardless of where they take place.

The one area where there can be no universal norms concerns the actual process of resolving ethical dilemmas. When problems arise, the individual in business has to look to his or her moral compass and apply it to the case at issue. That requires something more than asking whether others are doing a potentially questionable deed or whether the company has done the deed before. It calls for people to develop the habit of asking how a given course of action will affect others and assessing the various (often conflicting) interests affected by a decision. This is not easy because business managers and employees rarely have sufficient information to feel absolutely certain they are doing the right thing and decisions are often made under great pressure of time. Yet that is part of the discipline and excitement of business, which provides a constant testing ground for leadership in this area as in any other. In the next part of this chapter we look at three examples of people – an owner-manager, an expatriate middle manager and an investment bank employee – making their own ethical judgements in challenging circumstances.

CHOCOLATE FOR THE MILITARY

Sir Adrian Cadbury, pioneer of corporate governance in the UK and former chairman of the confectionery and soft drinks group Cadbury Schweppes, firmly believes that managers should make their own ethical rules. By way of illustration he tells two stories about his grandfather from the start of the 20th century when Cadbury was the second largest chocolate manufacturer in Britain. Queen Victoria wanted to give a decorative tin with a bar of chocolate inside to all her soldiers who were serving in the Anglo-Boer War in South Africa. This presented an ethical dilemma. While Sir Adrian's grandfather wanted more orders and additional work for his factory, he was deeply and publicly opposed to the war. He overcame the dilemma by accepting the order, but carrying it out at cost. In so doing he avoided making a profit from what he saw as an unjust war, his employees had the benefit of additional work and the soldiers received their royal present.

Yet Sir Adrian's grandfather's problems did not end there. Because he felt so strongly about the South African War, he had bought and financed the only British newspaper which opposed it. Because he was also against gambling, he tried to run the paper without any references to horse racing, which is an important driver of newspaper circulation. Since the commercial consequences were dire he was forced to choose between his ethical beliefs, deciding in the end that it was more important that his message about the war was heard as widely as possible than that gambling should thereby receive mild encouragement.

Sir Adrian draws a number of lessons. These anecdotes show, first, that the conflict between ethical and commercial considerations has long existed in business, though in an age where organised interest groups have become more vocal such conflicts attract much more critical attention than in the Victorian era. Second, the experience with the newspaper demonstrates that ethical signposts do not always point in the same direction. As suggested earlier, there is no simple, universal formula for solving ethical problems. We have to choose from our own codes of conduct whichever rules are appropriate to the case in hand. The outcome of such choices makes us who we are. Finally, while it is difficult to resolve dilemmas when our own rules of conduct conflict, the biggest problems arise when our decisions affect the interests of others. In practice, when that happens, a manager has to identify those who are affected and allocate weights to all the conflicting interests involved. This is rarely easy. If, for example, there is a conflict between shareholders and employees, there may be widely differing interests and views among different shareholders, while the manager may feel obliged to take into account the interests of potential employees as well as the existing workforce.[2]

UP THE CREEK IN BORNEO WITHOUT PETROL

The issues in the Cadbury example are, in one sense, less complex than those faced by many managers and employees on a day-to-day basis because Cadbury in 1900 was a family business. There was no need to reconcile a decision to reduce the company's profits with the interests and views of outside shareholders. Yet it does not follow that managers in quoted companies are unable to take decisions that deliberately eschew maximising profits for shareholders for ethical or corporate responsibility reasons. Charles Handy, the European management guru, has given an example from his own experience as a regional manager in a distant outpost of one of the big oil companies. A responsibility of his was to deal with the village of Kapit and its headman, 200 miles up the Rejang River in Borneo. One year there had been an unusually large crop of nuts and the tribes-people had loaded them into canoes powered by outboard motors and sped downriver to the merchants in Kapit. Handy had failed to anticipate their demand for petrol. The town was out of it and it would take a week for the steamer to come upriver with new supplies. Since the town had no space and no food for all these people, Handy was not the most popular or respected white man around and spent an uncomfortable few days.

To many economists and hard-nosed business folk this would have seemed a wonderful opportunity to exploit a monopoly position by trebling (or more) the price of the petrol when it arrived. There was no likelihood that a competitor would come in because the cost of entering this small market was prohibitive relative to any likely profits. Yet the thought never occurred to Handy. When the petrol did arrive he sold it at a 50 per cent discount to say he was sorry. His concern for his customers far outweighed any consideration of earnings per share. He was, he says, driven by his own self-respect, in which ethics no doubt played a part, and by the need to preserve his reputation as the company's representative.[3]

The lesson he draws is that in the real world of business it is producing things for people on time, in good condition and at a fair price that matters, without mucking up a decent town, upsetting the local government or taking unreasonable advantage of a short-term profit opportunity. The story is also a good illustration of reputational risk and the notion of the "licence to operate", a concept we return to in chapter 5 on investing and speculating. If a business fails to manage its relationship with the community properly it loses both reputation and legitimacy. A narrowly financial interpretation of shareholder value in such circumstances would ultimately have been destructive for everybody.

POKER AT SALOMON BROTHERS

In both these dramas the protagonists enjoyed considerable managerial autonomy. The businesses concerned also had solid reputations at the time. So consider, next, a very different example of an ethical dilemma at the other extreme – the dilemma that confronts employees rather than managers, in this case in an investment bank. This neck of the financial jungle is not noted for the passion of its ethical commitment, as the author Michael Lewis demonstrated in his best-selling book *Liar's Poker*. His account of what it was like to be recruited in the 1980s as a bond salesman at Salomon Brothers, together with the ethical dilemmas he confronted, is one of the wittiest things ever written about finance. But it also raises interesting questions. Of course, the book makes no claim to be a weighty tract and the stories are no doubt embellished. Yet this in no way detracts from their considerable merit as case studies.[4]

The first few months of anyone's career are often vital in establishing their attitudes to what behaviour is acceptable and unacceptable in the workplace. And it has to be said that an investment bank is one of the most difficult places in the world to make your own ethical rules. At Salomon Brothers the training course for new recruits sent a clear message that the trading floor was a free-for-all in which only the most competitive and ruthless would survive. A degree of ruthlessness was also expected of bond salesmen, for whom the ethical dilemmas centred on the fact that the relationship between the salesman and the client was often perceived to be zero-sum. That is, the dollar out of the client's pocket was a dollar in Salomon's pocket and vice versa. One of the difficulties of selling bonds, Lewis discovered, was persuading yourself that a bad idea for Salomon's own trading book was a good idea for a customer.

At the outset in Salomon's London business Lewis was given a handful of clients, institutional investors, who were too insignificant financially to matter to the firm if they were poorly treated and chose to take their business elsewhere. The ethical dilemma emerged just as he was congratulating himself on making the first sale of his career to a client he dubbed "Herman the German".

Herman wanted good ideas for profitable trades. And when Lewis returned to the office from lunch with the German he records that "a large corporate bond trader was waiting for me, like an unfed house pet". The trader had a great idea: AT&T (American Telephone and Telegraph) 30-year eurobonds had become cheap as measured against the benchmark 30-year US Treasury bond. He knew where he could put his hands on a few AT&Ts and suggested that Lewis tell his client to buy them at the same time as selling short 30-year US Treasury bonds. He promised that the client would come out of it well. What the trader failed to tell him was that these bonds had been on Salomon's trading books for months and the trader had been unable to get rid of them. Everyone in London apart from Lewis and the German had, it turned out, known that Salomon was desperate to unload the position. The bonds promptly went down in value. Herman the German's bank lost $60,000 while Salomon Brothers saved itself $60,000.

When Lewis remonstrated with the trader, the response was: "Who do you work for, this guy or Salomon Brothers?" The best thing he could do, says Lewis, after being so stupid as to trust a trader, was to pretend to others at Salomon that he had meant to screw the customer, because people would respect that – an interesting comment on the culture of what was then the pre-eminent bond house on Wall Street. When the extent of Herman the German's losses became known to his bosses, the unfortunate man, who had a pregnant wife, a new baby and a big home loan, was fired. On pondering how much guilt he felt shortly after doing the deal, Lewis drew the following lesson:

There was a convenient way of looking at this situation. My customer did not like his loss, but it was just as much his own fault as mine. The law of the bond market is caveat emptor. *That's Latin for "buyer beware". (The bond markets lapse into Latin after a couple of drinks.* Meum dictum pactum *was another Latin phrase I used to hear, but that was just a joke. It means "my word is my bond".) I mean, he didn't have to believe me when I told him AT&T bonds were a good idea.*

In time Lewis managed to find a way of running a streetwise moral conscience in the bond market. He finally became a "big swinging dick", in the argot of the trading floor, by peddling to a speculatively inclined French investor $86m-worth of bonds Salomon was desperate to unload for a client. He did so on the basis of extracting a promise from one of his bosses that Salomon would remove the bonds from Lewis's client's portfolio in due course, leaving him with a profit. But he still felt bad about placing his most cherished customer in jeopardy.

This demonstrates a surprisingly delicate sensibility for a bond salesman since he told no lies to his client about the nature of the investment and tried to take out an insurance policy for the client by extracting the promise from his boss. What the value of that promise really was – and Lewis did think it valuable – is hard for an outsider to judge. The irony is that if the promise was real this was a sale-or-return transaction on which it would have been incorrect to record a dealing profit at the time. Lewis does not say whether he revealed it to the Salomon accountants or internal auditors, but we somehow doubt that he did. Here was another case of the ethical signposts pointing in different directions.

Anyone who has been near a trading floor will recognise the accuracy of Michael Lewis's description of the behaviour there as well as the correct diagnosis of the conflicts of interest that arise. From our perspective, the interesting point about this last anecdote is that Lewis actually asks himself what is often a very good ethical question: am I putting my own interests and those of my firm before the interests of my client? He also comes up with a solution to the dilemma which, if somewhat unorthodox, relies on the sound ethical principle of seeking to mitigate the harm. It is, in fact, a good example of an individual making his own ethical rules. That was no mean feat for a bond salesman at Salomon Brothers in the 1980s.

Yet Lewis was actually asking the wrong question for one who was trading in a professional market dealing with an investor who probably had much more experience than he. (A novice fund manager would not have had authority to spend $86m on a single bond deal.) A lower order question would have served, such as: have I disadvantaged this client by withholding information or deceiving him in any way as to the nature and risks of the transaction? The answer was clearly not. As for the transaction with Herman the German, it was the trader, not Lewis, who perpetrated the deception. Lewis could not have disclosed the nature of the conflict of interest to his client – the traditional way of handling conflicts – because he was unaware of it. The lesson we draw – with apologies to Michael Lewis for putting his tale to high-minded examination – is that he was clearly right to seek a career in writing instead of sticking it out with Salomon Brothers. The combination of a reasonably normal moral conscience and an insufficient appetite for money making meant that he would never have been entirely at home in such a cut-throat world.

That said, it was not healthy for Salomon that such questioning behaviour was so atypical of the firm. The tone set at the top at that time was all about making as much money as possible and the devil take the hindmost. There were no bonuses for displaying ethical sensitivity. Some of Salomon's old guard, notably the respected economist Henry Kaufman, acted as the conscience of the firm. But by the end of the 1980s the ethos of greed was so embedded that no one in that position could have done anything to change the culture. Kaufman left to run his own advisory business. As so often when the tone at the top is wrong, the business soon went off the rails. In the early 1990s Salomon fell foul of the government for rigging the US Treasury bond market. It never really recovered from this scandal and was subsequently taken over by Citigroup, which in turn ran into one scandal after another in the United Kingdom, Europe and Japan. What took place on its trading floors was at odds with the values proclaimed by the board.

Among other things this demonstrates the difficulty of running a large organisation without solid ethical values, because values are the glue that holds an organisation together. That was one of the big lessons of Enron. The company trumpeted a set of values but then rewarded people who flouted them if the violation looked like boosting the bottom line. This was the case with Enron's online energy trading business which was developed at middle management level without the authorisation or knowledge of top management. Just before EnronOnline was launched in 1999 Sir Adrian Cadbury gave a lecture at London's Mansion House in which he said:

If unethical practices are ignored or condoned in a business, there is no means of knowing where the line between acceptable and unacceptable behaviour is to be drawn. The danger is that this uncertainty will result in a downwards slide in standards, which may become cumulative and end in disaster.

He could not have been more prescient. The high correlation between ethical failure and high-profile corporate collapses after the dotcom bubble makes an immensely powerful, practical case for business ethics. When it comes to the crunch, the character of a company really does matter.

VALUES OVER TIME, SCANDAL IN JAPAN

At the start of this chapter we raised the question of whether there are any absolute values in business that are applicable across the world. A related question is whether there is an ethical base in business that holds good for all time. It seems plausible that there have always been principles of fair dealing in markets because markets work more efficiently where there is trust and integrity. Yet perceptions of what is acceptable practice undoubtedly do change over time. The New Testament, for example, forbids lending at interest. But in due course Christianity shed this scruple while introducing laws against usury. Islam, in contrast, continues to prohibit lending at interest. More recently insider dealing, which used to be widely tolerated, has come to be perceived as unethical and is increasingly subject to legal restraints.

Such changes in perception often result from changes in economic circumstance. A revealing example of this concerns the relations between civil servants and businessmen in post-war Japan and the practice of *amakudari*. This is the so-called "descent from heaven" whereby top ministry officials customarily retire in their early 50s before the mandatory retirement age of 60 in order to take up lucrative posts at companies for which they had previously been responsible or had regulated and supervised. In the post-war period the close relationship between government and business was widely seen as one of the central elements of what was known as Japan Inc, the corporatist economic model that accompanied the Japanese economic miracle. Perceptions changed when the bubble economy of the 1990s burst and a series of governmental scandals rocked the country. The most colourful, as well as the most illustrative, was the *no pan shabu shabu* entertainment-for-favours scandal concerning visits by Ministry of Finance officials to the Lo Lan Chinese restaurant in Tokyo's Shinjuku entertainment district.

By way of background, the MoF at that time was regarded as the pinnacle of the Japanese governmental elite. Its premises were famously devoid of luxury and the culture was one of unstinting hard work. But there were perks to the job. Since much of the regulatory framework in post-war Japan gave a high degree of discretion to the bureaucrats, it was vital for companies to maintain good relations with their sponsoring ministry. So companies lavishly entertained top bureaucrats in the course of their civil service careers, who were subsequently compensated for their relatively low pay and hard work by the descent from heaven at the appropriate moment.

Shabu shabu was one of the perks, a hotpot dish of Japanese beef, while the *no pan* refers to the fact that the Lo Lan restaurant's big selling point was that the waitresses wore no pants. The officials at the heart of the scandal were Koichi Miyagawa and Toshimi Taniuchi, respectively the Ministry of Finance's chief bank inspector and his deputy. They and their underlings were regularly entertained by leading banks that they supervised, including most of the big names in Japanese finance. And in the course of the entertainment the officials leaked the times and locations of the MoF's inspections, which were supposed to be a surprise.

When this came to light, public anger was extreme because the post-bubble economy was in poor shape, unemployment was rising and people's savings had been badly eroded. One of the banks involved in the scandal, Hokkaido Takushoku Bank, went bust while others were weighed down by bad debts. The former ministry officials who plopped into comfortable jobs at the banks were seen to have failed, both in their regulatory role and in their subsequent role as managers in the private sector. This was most obviously so in the case of Hyogo Bank which was headed by a former director of the MoF's banking bureau when it collapsed in 1995 after spectacularly cooking the books to disguise the extent of its loan losses.

Such was the resentment over the entertainment-for-favours saga that the finance minister, Hiroshi Mitsuzuka, was forced to resign. *No pan shabu shabu* came to stand for everything, in the public perception, that was wrong with Japan's formerly much admired bureaucratic elite. Before he was taken into custody Miyagawa appeared on Japanese television where he declared that he did not believe he had allowed himself to be entertained "beyond acceptable social limits". He had clearly not grasped that the acceptable limit had changed. Another excuse was the purely practical one that the MoF's inspectorate was hopelessly understaffed and that if the banks had not been tipped off about inspections in advance, the job of sorting out the papers after a surprise entry would have taken so much time as to make the inspectors even less effective. Yet what passed in the bubble years was wholly unacceptable afterwards because the MoF was seen to have failed in both its economic and its regulatory roles. The story may also illustrate how the Japanese sense of ethics tends to be more goal oriented rather than driven by *a priori* norms because the public's ethical concern in the *no pan shabu shabu* affair was as much about the MoF's failure to meet its goals as a protest at the ethical lapses of the officials concerned.

To return to where we began, bribery and corruption are everywhere and always wrong. Yet the perception of what constitutes acceptable entertainment as opposed to an unacceptable bribe is clearly not immutable. There are invariably questions of definition and degree, which have to be addressed both by an organisation's or corporation's ethical code, and by individual judgement. No individual can be expected to exercise perfect judgement on every occasion.

NOTES

1   This is taken from *Moral Courage* by Rushworth M. Kidder (William Morrow, 2002). Kidder, a former columnist at the *Christian Science Monitor*, is the founder of the Institute for Global Ethics.

2   For a fuller account, see Sir Adrian Cadbury's essay *Ethical Managers Make Their Own Rules*, *Harvard Business Review*, 65: 5 (September–October 1987). It remains as relevant to the debate on business ethics today as it was then.

3   The story comes from the Michael Shanks Memorial Lecture, 1990, entitled *What is a Company For?*. It is reproduced in Charles Handy's book *Beyond Certainty* (Hutchinson, 1995).

4   Michael Lewis, *Liar's Poker: Two Cities, True Greed* (Hodder and Stoughton, 1989).

PART 2: Corporate Behaviour and Governance

Chapter 3

FIDUCIARIES

SPEED-READ SUMMARY

- Fiduciaries handle money on their clients' behalf. The rapid expansion of individual investors over the past 80 years has been primarily through fiduciaries such as collective investment vehicles, retail stockbrokers and financial advisers. Without fiduciaries, markets would be only for the brave and for financial professionals. Other representatives of individual investors such as lawyers and pension plan sponsors also have fiduciary responsibilities.

- The fiduciary industry depends on public credibility and it often puts down ethical abuses to the wayward actions of one bad apple. But abuses can become widespread when business models are susceptible to conflicts of interest.

- In this chapter we look at fiduciaries more generally and then focus on the most common financial fiduciary retail investors meet – the mutual fund.

- The Glass-Steagall Act of 1933 was passed partly in response to conflicts of interest that had emerged in the burgeoning mutual fund industry of 1920s' America. These conflicts re-emerged in the industry in the 1990s when commercial and political pressures removed the restrictions that Glass-Steagall had imposed.

- Case study: the market-timing and late-trading abuses carried out by Canary Capital Partners on the holders of Bank of America's Nations Funds was with the tacit support of certain employees at Bank of America and its subsidiaries.

Except when buying their home, individual investors rarely buy an investment directly, and even when they do, they often employ lawyers and agents to guide them through the process or represent them. Even if an investor avoids all fund management and advisory services, she will still need a broker who will execute investment trades, and she will still pay the broker a commission for these services. The presence of professional intermediaries who, one would hope, know what they are doing, and are subject to regulation, helps protect the non-professional customer and smooth the operation of markets. Markets that are well functioning, where investors feel relatively secure, are inclusive of a wider group of investors, making them bigger, more efficient and cheaper to use. But intermediaries, as the name suggests, get between an investor and their investment and many of them do not just guide their investor-clients through a transaction, they often handle client money. In doing so they are required to act on the client's behalf and in their best interests. They have what are referred to as fiduciary responsibilities and, unlike some middlemen, they play an important and needed role in complex businesses like finance and law.

By handling client money, a financial broker has an opportunity for fraud and abuse. This opportunity is greater the more discretion the broker or financial intermediary has on what he or she can do with your money. A "balanced" fund manager may have more discretion to act than a single country equity mutual fund manager, who in turn has more discretion than an "execution-only" broker. Those who handle client money directly and manage the finances of non-professionals are, not surprisingly, subject to the greatest regulation. (Though this can lead to the perverse situation where if your aunt Agatha has been persuaded by her neighbour to invest in his boat-building business as a private-equity investor, and there were no intermediaries involved, the transaction could easily escape the protection of the regulators.)

The main fiduciaries that individual investors come across are managers of collective investment vehicles such as mutual funds and pension funds. This chapter will focus on the ethics of mutual funds – a subject that has recently been much scrutinised following the market-timing and late-trading abuses that occurred between, 1998 to 2003. Many of these abuses took place in the United States, partly because the mutual fund industry is so much larger there than elsewhere. At the time of the scandals, almost $10 trillion of assets were managed on behalf of 95 million US customers.

FIDUCIARIES, ETHICS AND THE LAW

It became clear in 2002–2003 that ethical lapses at mutual funds had become widespread during the stock market boom of the 1990s. There is a parallel between what occurred this time around and the widespread ethical lapses in investment trusts during the 1920s that are well described in J. K. Galbraith's classic, *The Great Crash*.[1] The Glass-Steagall Act that followed those earlier abuses in 1933, tried to remove conflicts of interest in the industry that were seen as behind many of the abuses of the time. In the 1930s, the names engulfed in the investment trust scandals were leveraged trusts like Shenandoah and Blue Ridge (which was an investment trust that invested in investment trusts), both sponsored by Goldman Sachs.

This time around, well-known names such as Janus, Strong, Alliance, Putnam and Nations Funds found themselves accused of allowing favoured clients to gain returns at the expense of other mutual fund shareholders. By 2005 when much of the litigation was over, some 21 mutual fund businesses were named in prosecutions relating to the scandals, and 11 firms agreed to pay $3 billion in fines, restitution and reduced investment management fees. The two primary abuses, as mentioned above, were market-timing and late-trading. These abuses sound quite specific to mutual funds, but the essence of the contrivances are common to many breaches of fiduciary responsibility.

WHY THE ABUSES TOOK PLACE BETWEEN 1998–2003

You may ask, why was there such a plethora of market-timing and late-trading scandals in the five years to 2003 rather than ten, 20 or 30 years earlier? Part of the answer may appear to lie in the technology transformation and globalisation of markets, which

➤ P.42

■ Market-timing

Market-timing in the mutual fund industry means the quick buying and selling, normally within 24 hours, of a mutual fund's shares to take advantage of discrepancies between the fund's share price and the value of its underlying holdings. Foreign funds or locally registered funds of foreign stocks provide fertile ground for mis-pricings because of the different closing times between the US and foreign markets. A mutual fund of overseas stocks, registered in the US, closes at 4 p.m. Eastern Standard Time (EST), but the basis of a mutual fund's share price is the closing share prices of its holdings, which is likely to have been many hours earlier. Events after the closing of a foreign market, yet before the close in the US, may change the value of an underlying holding in a foreign market from its closing share price. This valuation change, however, may be reflected in out-of-hours trading in the foreign market, but it will not be reflected in the price of the US-based mutual fund until the foreign market opens the following day.

Consider a Japanese equity mutual fund registered in the United States. By Monday midday in the USA, the Tokyo stock exchange is long closed and the mutual fund's share price is determined. However, investors can still buy the mutual fund before 4 p.m. in New York. In essence, investors are able to buy a portfolio of Japanese stocks after the Japan market has closed at the closing price. Imagine that at 3:30 p.m. in NY on Monday a market-timer notices that the S&P 500 is up strongly for the day and, on average, this implies that Japanese stocks will open on Tuesday with an upward momentum. She buys the Japanese mutual fund until 4 p.m. NY time. The next day the Japanese stocks rise and close higher. Depending on the size of redemption and loading charges she faces, the market-timer may be able to sell the mutual fund at a tidy profit.

This is not a riskless bet. The Nikkei does not always follow the S&P and the Japanese mutual fund may own Japanese shares that follow the S&P even less closely than the average. But to paraphrase Eliot Spitzer, the New York State Attorney General, it is rather like being able to bet on a horse in the middle of a race, at the odds offered before the starting pistol was fired.

This just sounds clever on the part of the market-timer and silly on the part of the mutual fund regulations. But note three things. First, the person best able to market-time is the fund manager of the mutual fund who knows the underlying holdings and whether they are likely to follow the S&P or not. Although the main stock indices rose dramatically and in some correlation between 1996 and 2000, within the indices there were discrepancies in sector performance with "big-caps" (large firms) outperforming "small-caps" and "new-economy" sectors like information technology outperforming "old-economy" sectors like iron and steel and energy. If you owned a mutual fund specialising in "small-cap", old ➤

economy stocks in Japan, your mutual fund could consistently fall as the S&P 500 rose over this period. Fund managers and those they passed on information to on the underlying holdings of the funds they managed were those most frequently accused of market-timing.

Second, market-timing is often unprofitable because of redemption charges, which are often there in order to restrict market-timing or similar behaviour. These charges are sometimes waived for fund managers. Third, and this is a critical point from an ethical perspective, the profit of the market-timer in a mutual fund is only made at the expense of the other investors in the fund. In our example above, on Tuesday morning when the Tokyo stock market has reopened and the fund manager tries to add to the fund's holdings in order to satisfy the buy-order from the market-timer, the Tokyo market has opened higher as the market-timer hoped, and so the manager has to buy the fund's pool of stocks at higher prices than the mutual fund offered them to the market-timer the previous afternoon. The mutual fund manager had effectively sold stocks for less than he bought them at, and incurred a trading loss. This loss reduces the return of everyone else in the fund. The market-timer has had a gain, not at the expense of the market, but at the expense of the other holders of the fund.

■ Late-trading

Late-trading is similar to market-timing but different and related more to the trading in mutual funds based on local stocks. It refers to the practice of allowing favoured investors to buy or sell mutual fund shares at the 4 p.m. closing price, after 4 p.m. By regulation in the United States, the daily closing price is set at 4 p.m. Eastern Standard Time and anyone trading in mutual fund shares after 4 p.m. is required to receive the next day's price.

Market-moving corporate news is often held back until the market closes to minimise market disruption and to put retail and professional investors on a level playing field of information when the market reopens the following morning. A client armed with the knowledge of events occurring after the close and yet being able to buy a holding in the mutual fund at its closing price, may be able to book easy profits by using good indicators of the direction the market or certain stocks will open the next day.

For example, if General Motors were to announce at five minutes past 4 p.m that it had sold a troublesome subsidiary for a better than expected price, a late-trader would buy an "Autos fund" with a large exposure to GM, at the 4 p.m. price of the fund, in the expectation that come the following morning, that mutual fund's price would rise. If he is right, and he is exempt from redemption

➤

charges, the late-trader may then sell the mutual fund in the morning, booking a profit. Again, this is not risk-less. It is possible that the stock market would interpret the event differently than the late-trader and GM shares could fall, dragging down the mutual fund's share price. But the odds are stacked in the late-trader's favour. And as in market-timing, these easy profits are made at the direct expense of other shareholders in the mutual fund. Those most frequently charged with allegations of late-trading were brokers, or those who set themselves up as brokers, as they were often exempt from redemption charges.[2]

made these abuses easier. We doubt this was a major factor however. Edwin Lefèvre describes in another investment classic *Reminiscences of a Stock Operator*, first published in 1925, how operators in regional stock markets would take advantage of market-timing factors to make a tidy profit in the early 1900s.[3] Market-timers could be just as effective in the age of the ticker tape as in the age of broadband. Part of the answer, as we discuss at greater length in chapter 10 on bankers, is that when markets are rising as in 1998 to 2000 and everyone is making money, market participants tend to turn a blind eye to activity that later, when markets have crashed and many are nursing losses, appears obviously unfair. A main part of the answer too, lies in the changing ownership structure of the industry and in its corporate governance arrangements.

After the Glass-Steagall Act in 1933 to around the mid-1970s, mutual fund managers tended to be small, privately owned professional firms that saw themselves exclusively as fiduciaries of other people's money. Their business depended on their reputation and so it made little business sense for mutual funds to try and put their own corporate interests before those of the investors. But as John Bogle, founder and former CEO of The Vanguard Group, a mutual fund owned by its members, has put it:

Over the years funds became big business. Managers sold their shares to the public and many became part of giant financial conglomerates. Amassing assets under management became the fund industry's primary goal and our focus gradually shifted from stewardship to salesmanship. The principle of long-term investing in highly diversified equity funds morphed into short-term speculation in ever more aggressive specialised funds. Portfolio turnover for the average fund went right through the roof, soaring from the 15 per cent range in the 1950s (a six-year holding period for the average stock) to 110 per cent last year, an average holding period of just eleven months. We were no longer an own-a-stock industry. We were a rent-a-stock industry, a world away from Warren Buffett's favourite holding period: forever.

The changes in mutual fund management and the move towards financial conglomeration created conflicts of interest between the fund managers and the shareholders whose funds they managed. For example, most mutual fund managers are paid on the basis of the size of assets under management. They are therefore under constant temptation to let their funds grow beyond the point where it may be difficult for the investor to implement strategies quickly, which ultimately undermines their investment performance. It is interesting to note that where managers are paid on the basis of performance and have substantial personal stakes in the funds they manage, they have from time to time done the unusual thing of "giving back" money to investors claiming that their funds had grown too large to manage optimally.

It also became fashionable in today's fund business model to bring out new, and often speculative funds with untried strategies to capitalise on the fads and fashions of the markets. This is good for business, but often bad for investors. And in financial conglomerates, there is a temptation for managers to favour clients who could provide lucrative business for other parts of the conglomerate, even where it disadvantaged the other mutual fund shareholders. This last factor played an important role in the late-trading abuses.

Ultimately, the trouble with the new hard-driven business orientation of mutual funds is that the industry's traditional governance arrangements were playing catch-up with the new principal/agent conflicts that were being created between managers and investors. At the time of the scandals, the two were often fused. The chairman of the mutual fund, representing the investors, was often also representing the shareholders of the management company. This conflict of interest was often present all the way through the organisation to the fund managers and risk managers. The regulatory authorities, as is so often the case, were too slow to scrutinise the implications of the changing profile of mutual fund companies and the resulting conflicts. In the US, the Securities and Exchange Commission failed to take note, even when late-trading and market-timing abuses became commonplace during the dotcom boom.

● Case study:
CANARY CAPITAL PARTNERS

One of the most publicised allegations of abuse was the apparent preferential treatment given by Bank of America's (BoA) mutual fund, Nations Funds, and broker dealer subsidiaries controlled by Edward Stern, who ran Canary Capital Partners LLC, a hedge fund. At the end of legal investigations into their involvement in late-trading and market-timing abuses, on 15 March 2004, BoA and Fleet Boston (who were in the process of merging) agreed to pay fines and charges amounting to $675 million as final settlement. No wrongdoing was accepted or denied, though this was the largest single fine in the mutual fund scandal.

We use this example and others throughout the book neither to reopen investigations – we provide no information that has not been in the public domain for some time – nor to single out these companies for blame. These events took place in the past. Many others were similarly tarnished, and those that were tend to have made the most corrective changes. Our purpose is to learn from what allegedly happened in order to help individuals in similar situations in the future. Consequently, for this exercise we assume the worst of what was alleged did take place and look at the questions that, had they been asked, might have helped to avoid it. Throughout this book we take a simple view that many essentially honest individuals and institutions committed ethical abuses that, on greater reflection in the cold light of day, perhaps with some guidance via a few simple questions, they would normally have recoiled against. It is noteworthy that throughout the alleged abusive behaviour, the marketing slogan of BoA was "higher standards".

In May 2002, the Board of BoA approved a 2 per cent redemption fee for investors who sold Nations Funds' international funds over a period of less than 90 days after purchase. The move was designed to maintain the ability of long-term investors to liquidate their holdings quickly (they wouldn't end up paying the fee) while discouraging investors using these funds as vehicles for market-timing (who would). BoA's mutual funds also separately enforced the standard prohibition against late-trading. Investors who put in orders to buy or sell mutual fund shares after 4 p.m. could receive only the next day's closing value of the fund. In these actions, the very top management of BoA showed that they understood the potential and harm of market-timing and late-trading abuses and they established clear rules to prevent them. With the wonderful vision of hindsight the same managers could have been more circumspect in delegating issues of monitoring and enforcing these rules.

Although late-trading was illegal under the prevailing regulations, it had become normal practice in the industry to offer today's 4 p.m. price for orders from agents that came in a few hours after 4 p.m. The thinking behind the practice was that for large mutual funds with many agents selling the funds across a wide geography, the process of gathering the orders and delivering them to the mutual fund is not instantaneous. An order made by the end-investor at 3:30 p.m. without any intention of late-trading, but made through an agent, may only reach the mutual fund a couple of hours later.

From mid-1998 to 2003, employees at Nations Funds gave Edward Stern of Canary Capital Partners (a hedge fund) an electronic terminal that allowed him, like an agent, to enter orders until 6:30 p.m. at the 4 p.m. price. Nations Funds were not alone in doing so. Mr Stern also used a platform provided by the Security Trust Company to make post-4 p.m. trades at 4 p.m. prices at other mutual funds offered by, for example, Bank One, Janus Capital and Strong Capital Management. Employees at Nations Funds further allowed Mr Stern to buy and sell their international funds without being subject to the 2 per cent charge on those who buy and sell within 90 days. It is alleged that employees of Nations Funds also gave him detailed current information on the funds' holdings that was not generally available to others, and bankers at BoA sold him a basket option that enabled him to short the portfolio of stocks owned by the fund.

At 4 p.m. each day, Mr Stern could buy a basket option from BoA that allowed him to go short the stocks in a Nations Funds international mutual fund. If he learned at 6 p.m. that international stocks were moving up and so the fund value would be likely to rise the next day, he could neutralise his short-position by buying the fund at 6:30 p.m. at 4 p.m. prices. If however international stocks were falling, he could hope to profit from his option position. Mr Stern was put in a privileged position. It did not bring certain rewards, but substantially fixed the odds in his favour. Given the specific products that BoA and its subsidiaries apparently either sold or provided to Mr Stern, it would be reasonable to assume, especially in the age of "know your customer" and "leveraging client relationships across the organisation" that someone at BoA knew what he was doing.

Another way of looking at this is that Mr Stern received privileged information from sources within Nations Funds to decide whether to hedge the option position he bought from BoA, or not, and when this information indicated that he should hedge, the late-trading transaction Nations Funds allowed effectively transferred the likely loss of the option to the unsuspecting holders of the fund. The financial loss was spread over so many other holders that it was hardly noticeable to anyone other than Mr Stern.

In the subsequent resolution of the official investigation, Mr Stern agreed to pay fines and charges amounting to $40 million. This is the equivalent of the management fees Canary Capital Partners made over this period. This is likely to have been a fraction of the gains made by investors in the Canary Capital Fund including Mr Stern personally.

Mr Stern's late-trading and market-timing were apparently not curbed until the New York State Attorney General's office issued a subpoena to the Nations Funds in July 2003. (Mr Stern's strategy of shorting the mutual fund with the mutual fund holders underwriting any loss was very lucrative during the large and long stock market decline from 2001 to 2003.) At the heart of the problem was that, standing back and looking at all of the related companies as single ones, BoA was making money selling products to Canary Capital Partners that enabled Canary to take performance away from holders of BoA's family of mutual funds. The alleged motivation for BoA's actions was that the bank may have reasonably expected other business from Mr Stern given that his family's estimated worth was in excess of $3 billion and his related companies were active market participants. It is important to point out that the allegations against BoA do assume that companies operate with a degree of co-ordination and communication between their subsidiaries that is not always present.

This case appears to be a classic example of a conflict of interest that had arisen through the ownership structure of the mutual fund – a structure commonplace throughout the industry. It was the type of conflict that was prevalent in the 1920s and led to the passing of the Glass-Steagall Act in 1933. Regulatory enforcement actions after the abuses and separate action by the funds, including Nations Funds, have tried to recreate some separation between the management and ownership of mutual funds. It is possible that this conflict would have been avoided if Glass-Steagall had been updated rather than replaced by the Gramm-Leach-Bliley Act of 1999 which eliminated various restrictions between commercial and investment banks, and allowed banks to provide a wider range of services than previously allowed. That perspective comes with some hindsight.

CONCLUSION AND THE QUESTIONS THAT SHOULD HAVE BEEN ASKED

The mutual fund scandal ended up costing the protagonists a larger amount in fines and disgorgements than the scandals associated with analyst conflicts of interest in the sale of IPOs. Yet they appear to feature less prominently in the public folklore than the puffing of dotcom stocks, the IPO abuses and, of course, the scandals surrounding Enron, WorldCom and Parmalat. This is a little odd, as the individuals at the centre of the scandals appear to have committed less ambiguous ethical breaches than in each of these other cases and with even less of a blush. Each of the key ethical concerns we describe in this book is on display in this scandal: conflicts of interest, contrivances that put favoured clients at an advantage to others and unmitigated harm to some of those implicitly involved in the transactions.

A further concern that we repeat throughout this book is the devolving of ethical responsibility. The Canary–Nations Funds case that we have focused on in this chapter took place through a series of connected companies, on both sides of the transaction, yet it is unclear whether any single individual or two masterminded the contrivance across BoA and its subsidiaries. This may be important from a legal perspective, but we believe it is less important from an ethical perspective. Those involved with specific parts of the overall transaction had a responsibility to themselves, their firm and their clients to join up the dots and question the veracity of the transactions. In a moment, we turn to the questions that they should have asked.

We have made a distinction between legal and ethical responsibilities above but arguably it was also in the long-term self-interest of the funds that employees went beyond their legal responsibilities. Although the business models have changed, the value of a mutual fund brand continues to rest on the trust of its clients. Putnam, for instance, suffered a $21 billion outflow of client money when market-timing abuses there came to light. As the scandals unfolded, Morningstar, which analyses funds' performance and ranks them, advised investors to consider selling a range of mutual funds, not for performance reasons, but because of their ethical deficit in looking after the interests of fund holders. These funds included not just Nations Funds, but also Janus, Alger, Alliance Bernstein, One Group and Strong, some of the heavyweights of the industry. (Putnam was excluded from Morningstar's list because by the time the list was published it had made a number of corrective actions.) In time all of those named initiated corrective actions.

The financial industry likes to portray abuses as the result of one bad apple that has since been thrown out. But the mutual fund scandals involved 21 different firms. In part, many mutual fund managers were swept along by the instant-gratification culture that generally prevailed at the time and was, if anything, validated by the large, short-term, performance-related remuneration packages at the very top of these organisations. This does not excuse the behaviour of individuals lower down the organisation hierarchy. But it does suggest that if department managers had paused to ask themselves a few basic questions, the abuses might have been more easily recognisable and less widespread and persistent. They would also have saved themselves and their businesses the consequences.

➤ QUESTIONS THAT SHOULD HAVE BEEN ASKED

1.   Do I have a disguised conflict of interest?

Mutual fund managers' primary duty of care is to the investors – shareholders of the mutual funds. Late-trading and market-timing directly undermine the interests of these holders. To permit this behaviour in order furtively to advantage the fund managers or favoured clients was not illegal, but it is a clear conflict of interest.

2.   Have I created some contrivance that puts myself, or my partners, at some advantage to others (or put others at some disadvantage)?

Selling Canary Capital Partners a basket option to short the stocks in a BoA mutual fund, and then allowing Canary two and a half hours after the official closing price to decide whether to neutralise the short or not, was not banned within the operational rules at the time. But it was clearly a contrivance carried out by a handful of individuals at BoA-related companies, designed to give Canary Capital Partners an advantage not generally offered. The purpose of the contrivance was to profit Canary Capital Partners and employees of BoA, who may reasonably have expected to be rewarded through other related dealings.

3.   Am I causing unmitigated harm to any of the stakeholders touched by this transaction?

Many people believe that equality of treatment should be an important principle, but while we are well disposed to this principle, we are not certain that it should be an overriding one. In finance, many individuals come from different vantage points and treating them equally could be inappropriate, unfair or commercially unsound. It would be inappropriate to treat a wealthy hedge fund manager with 30 years of professional experience in the same way as a pensioner

➤

investing his or her life savings with little financial experience. We are more concerned about conflicts, contrivances and whether we are causing unmitigated harm. In the case of market-timing and late-trading, profits were made by a privileged few, at the direct expense of those not-so-favoured.

In the immediate aftermath of the scandals, it is our impression that these questions are increasingly being asked in the mutual fund industry, perhaps no more closely today than during the Nations Funds case and by those others engulfed by the scandals at the turn of the 21st century. The value of asking these questions will be apparent when those who have observed the scandals from first hand move on or retire and new kids on the block are wondering how best to hit their bonus targets.

NOTES:

1   J. K. Galbraith, *The Great Crash 1929*, Reprint edition (Mariner, 1997).

2   The definitions of market-timing and late trading borrow heavily from the definitions set out by Christopher Wright in his article "I Knew It Was Wrong But I Did It Anyway", Ethics Forum, *CFA Magazine* (Jan–Feb 2004).

3   Edwin LeFèvre, *Reminiscences of a Stock Operator*, 1923 (Traders, 1985).

Chapter 4

MIS-SELLING & INVESTOR PROTECTION

SPEED-READ SUMMARY

- The principle of caveat emptor is inappropriate in retail financial markets because products are often complex, lacking in transparency and prone to conflicts of interest. Mis-selling has been rife all around the world.

- A paternalistic approach to advising investors has given way to a more profit-oriented culture in selling financial services. The bankers' fiduciary obligation to look after clients' interests has come into conflict with the short-term interests of bank shareholders.

- The UK offers an extreme case where mis-selling has become so endemic that public confidence in financial service providers has been eroded.

- At the root of the problem is the failure to align the incentives offered to the sales force with the interests of customers. Regulators have had mixed success in addressing this fundamental flaw in the way the retail financial services industry operates.

In wholesale markets where professionals are dealing with other professionals the principle of *caveat emptor* – let the buyer beware – is usually a sensible basis on which to conduct business. Retail financial markets are another matter because retail financial products are often complex and lacking in transparency. As we noted in chapter 1, the buyers often cannot know for years whether the product is sound or flawed. So they can be easily put at a disadvantage vis-à-vis the seller. In a market bedevilled by information asymmetry, to use the economist's jargon, conflicts of interest abound. It is not surprising, then, that there have been countless examples across the world in recent years of mis-selling – rip-offs, in plain language – which amount to a flagrant abuse of fiduciary responsibility. These have ranged from the sale of products by British and continental European banks that were unsuitable for the clients' tax or pension circumstances, to the peddling of home loans in an overheated Korean property market to very young people whose ability to service the loans was known to the lending bankers to be questionable.

BEWARE OF HINDSIGHT

It is worth emphasising at the outset that the ethical questions raised by these mis-selling episodes are not always as clear cut as the scandalised media coverage implies. Too often, hindsight enters into the equation, together with the mentality that if anyone incurs a loss on their investment someone must be to blame. A good example of this was the sale in Japan of variable life insurance policies. These policies have caused much grief to homeowners who were persuaded to mortgage their houses and invest the proceeds in an insurance policy in the hope of avoiding high inheritance taxes. The salespeople are alleged to have failed to explain that the payouts, far from being guaranteed, were related to the value of the investments in the policy. When Japan's notorious stock market and property bubbles burst at the turn of the millennium, policyholders found that they owed more on their mortgages than the surrender value of their policies. Trillions of yen were lost, many faced eviction, several committed suicide and the wider public was deeply shocked.

On the face of it, this looks like a case of cynical and unscrupulous salesmanship. Yet in reality, in the bubble economy period in the late 1980s when the policies were first sold, scarcely anyone in Japan believed that the stock market would cease to rise. The nature of a bubble is precisely that almost everyone is caught up in the general euphoria. During the bubble there was a pervasive sense even among sophisticated financial people that levitation in asset prices was the norm. So it was hindsight that turned this selling into mis-selling. The outcome was undoubtedly unfortunate for the policyholders involved, but the story is more one of the horrific consequences of a bubble than of a conscious and deliberate attempt to rip-off the Japanese public. The salespeople were taken in by the bubble along with their customers. They thought they were selling a lower risk product than was actually the case. But in the aftermath of the bubble a blame culture very understandably set in, just as it did after the South Sea Bubble, the Mississippi Bubble and the 1929 crash. The Japanese public looked for a scapegoat.

That said, there has been a plethora of genuine scandals where hindsight is not an issue and unethical behaviour most certainly is. As with the market-timing and late-trading abuses described in chapter 3, the fact that such scandals appear to have become more frequent reflects profound changes in the structure of the financial services market. Fifty years ago in the US and Europe people who needed financial advice turned instinctively to their bank manager, who was a respected member of the community with good local knowledge. He – and it invariably was a he – would steer a client away from one product towards another even if doing so would lead to a lesser profit for the bank. This approach to banking was tinged with paternalism, but the underlying assumption was that selling a product that was right for the client's personal circumstances regardless of its profitability for the bank was in the long-run interests of the bank and its shareholders as well as those of the client.

Everything changed in the 1980s with the shareholder value revolution. People in quoted companies from the chief executive officer down came under much greater pressure to increase earnings on an annual, half yearly and quarterly basis. The result was that the bankers' fiduciary obligation to look after the client's interest came into potential conflict with the short-term interest of shareholders. The conflict was greatly exacerbated by the introduction of sales targets and incentive rewards for employees, together with stock option and other equity-related awards. With the introduction of mass marketing and high-powered sales teams the bank manager ceased to be an important figure. His clients metamorphosed into mere customers whom modern bankers depersonalise by calling them the customer base. Against that background some CEOs and many salespeople made a rational calculation that they could profitably mistreat customers by selling them inappropriate products.

THE UK – AN EXTREME CASE

Among the worst hit by such unethical behaviour has been the UK, where financial rip-offs are so endemic that the public went through a period of being averse to saving for retirement through conventional pension products peddled by banks, insurance companies and other pension providers. Research by the Association of British Insurers has shown that at the time of writing around 8 million workers were not saving at all for retirement, while 2 million more were not saving enough. This partly reflects the disincentive effect of means-testing, whereby the less well off risk forfeiting their savings if they have to fall back on means-tested income support from the government in their retirement. But for the better off there are also understandable grounds for caution in the light of a succession of scandals over a 20-year period starting in the mid-1980s. The first of these came after Margaret Thatcher's Conservative administration decided to pass more of the pensions burden on to the private sector. The government provided incentives, in the form of a rebate of national insurance contributions, for people to buy personal pension plans. The target market was supposed to be those without adequate pension cover. Yet some 500,000 individuals out of the 2 million who bought personal pensions between 1988 and 1994 were persuaded by commission-driven salesmen to leave occupational pension funds. Of these, 90 per cent received inappropriate advice because they were not alerted to the high costs associated with transferring out of an occupational scheme, nor to the fact that they would forfeit the employer's contribution to their fund. For many others who bought personal pensions high commission charges ate up much of the investment return.

Banks and insurance companies were fined a total of £11 million as a result and the regulatory regime was tightened. Britain's Financial Services Authority has estimated that when all the potential cases of mis-selling have finally been reviewed compensation to policyholders will total nearly £12 billion. Yet despite this debacle the scandals kept coming, notably in endowment-related home loans where the borrowers were expecting to pay off their mortgage with the proceeds of an endowment policy that had been invested in the stock market. By mid-2004 more than three-quarters of endowment policies taken out to pay off mortgages were falling well short of their target and some big endowment providers such as Standard Life and Friends Provident admitted to falling short by more than 90 per cent. Once again it turned out that the salespeople had been putting heavy pressure on customers to buy a riskier product than they needed, often without explaining the risk, because they stood to earn more money than on selling a plain vanilla mortgage. At the time of writing the UK financial services watchdog has forced 24 companies to pay out £700 million in compensation.

Next came scandals related to structured products such as high yield bonds. These offered an enticing rate of interest, but without any capital guarantee. They were known to the sellers, though not to the customers, as "precipice" bonds because the investor's capital returns fell off a cliff if the markets sank below set trigger points. In many cases the money was invested at the turn of the millennium in risky telecom and dotcom stocks. Once again flawed incentive structures encouraged salespeople to sell products that were often unsuitable for the customer and without properly explaining the risks.

Perhaps it was no coincidence that the bank that suffered the largest ever fine for mis-selling at that point was the one that had pioneered the shareholder value revolution in the UK banking system: Lloyds TSB. It was fined £1.9 million over the sale of 22,500 policies through its branches in 2000 and 2001. No less than 44 per cent of these policies were unsuitable for the investors to whom they were sold. The bank had set aside £300 million to cover potential redress for customers, having earlier set aside at least £800 million to cover pensions mis-selling. It had also been obliged to pay compensation and heavy fines in relation to endowment policies and unit trusts. Yet these regulatory sanctions do not appear to have had a great impact on the behaviour of the management or branch staff. For in 2005 a BBC television documentary revealed more evidence of mis-selling. The programme makers had laid their hands on internal Lloyds documents which said that staff all across the branch network were paying little attention to customers' circumstances. Training, according to the leaked documents, was having little impact on staff behaviour and details of prospective borrowers' incomes and spending were being manipulated to achieve the best outcome for bonus-hungry Lloyds advisers with the needs of the customer and the bank taking second place to that objective.

A FAILURE OF REGULATION

The ethical lapses in the British financial services business since the mid-1980s have been on such an epic scale that they have done serious damage to the whole savings market. A notable feature is that reputational risk, transparency and fines imposed by the UK Financial Services Authority seem to have done little to constrain the directors, managers and employees of the biggest financial institutions. Why, in a business supposedly rooted in trust, did so many forget their fiduciary obligations to the point of comprehensively putting their own interests before those of the client?

The answer, as Sir Callum McCarthy, head of the FSA, has publicly recognised lies in the poor alignment of interests between those in the financial services business and the customers they were supposed to serve. There were powerful incentives for both managers and employees to put their own interests first and mistreat the customers. And that makes a broader and more fundamental point about what has gone wrong with business ethics: there can be no hope of maintaining or developing an ethical culture in a business if the incentive structures militate against "doing the right thing". A further point about the non-alignment of interests relates to the life of the product and the timing of bonuses. For if bonuses are awarded to salespeople at the beginning of the product's life instead of the end, they have little direct financial interest in whether the product serves the customer well over time.

This in turn raises important questions about the nature and role of regulation. When the British mis-selling scandals started in the 1980s' self-regulation was still a feature of parts of the financial system. In a community where there is a high level of trust, self-regulation can be very effective. It operates through peer pressure, like a club, with the ultimate sanction for wrongdoers being ejection from the club. The risk with this approach is that if there are no independent outsiders keeping an eye on what takes place in the club, the insiders lose touch with reality, as happened at the Lloyd's of London insurance market. Nor can it work if a market is opened up to a large number of new members who may not share the club values or whose presence undermines the solidarity of the club. That is one reason why financial regulation in the UK had to be substantially rethought at the time of the Big Bang on the London stock exchange in 1986, which permitted foreigners to buy up British securities firms. And as Sir Howard Davies, a former head of the Financial Services Authority, has remarked, while self-regulation is quite good at dealing with bad apples, it has not been good at raising standards in the market as a whole or in dealing with a problem where a whole industry needed to change.

Yet in shifting to a more formal kind of regulation the UK experience offers other lessons. The chief one is the importance of calibrating the carrots and sticks that drive human behaviour. As we have seen in relation to the carrots, if people are offered bonuses for short-term sales performance they will inevitably tend to put their own interests before those of customers with the result that the whole culture of the industry becomes tainted. As for the sticks, the fines imposed by the UK authorities did not hurt the employees who did the mis-selling and were not levied personally on the directors of the companies concerned. For the shareholders they were mostly too small to be a matter of consequence. Since mis-selling took place all across the industry, naming and shaming directors could not be used as a very effective sanction. To make a difference watchdogs need to take more draconian action along the lines pursued by the New York Attorney General Eliot Spitzer with aberrant investment banks; or of the Japanese Financial Services Agency, which in 2005 forced Citigroup of the US to close a private banking subsidiary which had violated Japanese mutual fund and securities laws and failed to look after its clients' interests properly. The overall message is that without a judicious combination of both carrot and stick, ethical behaviour is unlikely to flourish.

► **QUESTIONS FOR EXECUTIVES AND NON-EXECUTIVE DIRECTORS**

1. Are the incentives offered to the sales force or to intermediaries in tune or at odds with the fiduciary obligation to the clients?

2. Do the marketing practices of the organisation give rise to potential conflicts of interest that could pose reputational risks?

3. Does the *modus operandi* of the sales force serve the long-term interests of the shareholders?

► **QUESTIONS FOR SALESPEOPLE AND INTERMEDIARIES**

1. Are you putting your own financial interests before those of the clients?

2. Is the product you are promoting appropriate for the financial and tax circumstances of the client?

3. Are you satisfied you really understand the degree of risk that is appropriate for the client and that your advice reflects this?

Chapter 5

INVESTING & SPECULATING

SPEED-READ SUMMARY

- Investment in the hope of greater returns is the lifeblood of economic activity and should be welcomed, but it needs to be governed by good ethical practices or trust and markets will break down.

- As a result of failed speculative ventures throughout history, the law is often close on the heels of unethical and dubious practices, and the gap between what is unethical, yet also legal, has closed considerably.

- However, there is still an important distinction. In this chapter, we discuss Talisman Energy's investment in Sudan, Citigroup's €12.8 billion European government bond trade and touch on short selling, all of which raise serious ethical considerations, but none of which are/were clearly illegal.

- Given the wide variety of what investors can invest in, from prisons to new churches, ethical considerations in investment are far broader than in other financial activities, such as financial analysis or advice.

- Though not a substitute for appropriate controls, we believe that if investors more frequently reflect on the ethics of their actions, it would lead us to a better place than mere codes or more prescriptive regulations.

Is speculation the second oldest profession? The images conjured up by the word are many and most are unsavoury. Early 18th-century London saw unscrupulous brokers in Exchange Alley "pumping and dumping" stocks. Jay Gould was a legendary 19th-century robber baron who bought up cheap tracks of railways in Midwest America in such a way as to block his competitors from building a network, and then later, sold them to the same competitors for a small fortune. Pierpont Morgan developed an enviable reputation as a banker, whose word was his bond, but when deal-making, he was not above contrivances that put his competitors at a disadvantage if they got in his way. The adjective most frequently coupled with speculator is greedy. If you have several speculators, then it is often infectious greed. Defining a speculator as one who makes a bargain or invests a sum in the hope or belief that he or she would obtain a major reward, creates a fine dividing line between a "speculator" with its louche overtones and a "risk taker" with its more enterprising chime.

Many lauded explorers were speculators. Alexander Bell speculated in new technologies. Charles Darwin's development of evolutionary theory or Aryabhata's discovery that the Earth spins, could be described as intellectual speculators risking much for their pioneering departures from tradition, while Lord Keynes learned a fair amount of his economics from speculating on the stock market. These individuals took gambles and took steps to profit when the gambles paid off. If the rewards, in the widest sense of the word, to commercial risks are absent, few risks would be taken and economies would grind to a halt.

Risk taking in investment is not easily separated from risk taking in speculation. This is easily seen in the case of patents. Offering inventors a period in which they can "make hay" from their invention, free from the competition of copies, encourages invention. Public morality about speculation is often associated with the degree of toil and sweat that is involved in a speculation. The hard-working scientist who makes a medical discovery, late in life, and sells the idea to an investor for a comfortable retirement, is the honest risktaker. If the young investor strikes a hard bargain, for fear of buying a dud, and then strikes gold with the new product, he or she is then considered the greedy speculator. The investor, who buys and holds on to some stocks for ten years, is seen as a "good" long-term investor. But the investor who makes the same return by short-selling the stock of a company that he or she is convinced has made a bad investment is viewed as an evil speculator. Both types of investors are required for the efficient running of a market economy. We are sceptical that the amount and speed with which money is made or lost should be an important consideration (though we note that periods where quick money making appears easy are ripe with ethical abuses). The judgemental issue should be the nature of the bargain and its expected outcome. Even with a narrow view of ethics, the opportunities for unethical speculation are boundless.

That said, unethical speculation often leaves victims with tangible hurt. Consequently, speculation is an area where laws are plentiful, and in many ways legislators have sought for some time to make what they consider to be unethical speculation unlawful. We are not sure that such a distinction between ethical and unethical speculation is so clear as to be easily codified. Below we discuss where the distinction now lies between law and ethics in speculation, we then turn to examining why we need ethics when investing with two case studies. We conclude with a discussion of corporate social responsibility and the questions investors should asked themselves when faced with an ethical dilemma.

SPECULATION AND THE LAW

Behind the large mass of financial regulation and laws, the principal objectives are of modest ambition. Financial regulation is principally designed to protect both the integrity of financial markets and consumers from sharp practices. The main instruments of the law are disclosure requirements and the separation of players into broad categories. There are "insiders" and "outsiders" and market professionals and non-market professionals. To protect markets, the insiders – people with privileged financial information such as those involved in the acquisition of one company by another – are not permitted to take financial advantage of their information by trading in the markets. This prohibition often extends to their family, friends and colleagues. To protect consumers, financial products cannot be sold to non-market professionals without meeting strict criteria on who does the selling and how the sale is presented. (Which, incidentally, is why so many documents that are written to encourage you to buy a financial product have, in most jurisdictions, the small print at the bottom which says: "this is not an offer for sale".)

Proponents argue that a market rife with insiders and sharp practice will intimidate others who fear being at a disadvantage. This keeps markets smaller, less liquid and more costly to transact in than otherwise – itself a disservice to investors, savers and the wider economy. There is some research that the size of financial markets relates to the enforcement of rules that reduce the advantages of "insiders" over "outsiders".[1] It is debatable whether these are good or bad interventions by the lawmakers. Opponents of rules against insider trading and mis-selling argue that it creates disincentives for individuals to find information for themselves. Financial markets depend critically on healthy information markets. Where inside information is part of a contrivance to disadvantage others, it is, in our minds, more clearly unethical.

Where legal yet unethical behaviour is uncovered, as in some recent corporate scandals, the legislation often adapts to make it illegal. If the law is always reactive why should we expect more from financiers than legal behaviour? It is worth remembering that the scandals at Enron and WorldCom released a storm of moral indignation, but much of what happened was considered to be legal when applying the laws of the time.

WHY ETHICS?

We have discussed in chapter 1 of this book the need for ethical standards that are wider than the laws of the day. However, as we have seen above, laws relating to speculation are so all-encompassing that it is worth revisiting the issue. Do we need ethics? In the realm of financial speculation it would appear that the gap between what is illegal and what is merely unethical is very narrow. This is because of the recent adoption of very broad and non-absolute tests. For example, in many jurisdictions disrupting the market is illegal (even if done unintentionally) where disruption is often defined as whatever would be considered disruption by a regular market participant. An example of this approach to disruption is taken in the UK by the FSA. However, while this has closed the ethical gap *ex ante*, it has not closed the gap *a priori*. This broad and relativist definition of disruption provides a clearer picture of the legality of a behaviour after it has happened than before the disruption has occurred. It is not a direct disincentive to disruption – merely a punishment if both successful and caught.

A good example of this is the case of the Citigroup government bond trader's August 2004 trade. It is alleged that Citigroup traders intentionally planned to exploit weaknesses in the MTS electronic market in European government bonds by first placing a massive sell order and, when the market had fallen, buying a chunk back and thus making a significant profit (see case study p.66). Selling and buying back after the price has fallen is not an uncommon practice among traders. It was the scale of the operation and its destabilising effect on the market that singled it out for concern. The trade was only unreasonable in the context of its eventual impact. Whatever their intentions, the traders' behaviour could and was considered reasonable, even brave, by their peers. They may even have been uncertain as to the magnitude of the effect of the trade given that the MTS market was considered to be highly liquid. While we would consider this trade unethical for reasons we will discuss in a moment, its alleged contravention of the trading rules relates to its impact. If the intention was the same but there was no impact on market prices, it is unlikely that even if it became known, the question of legality would have been pursued as rigorously as it was. Yet surely an action is not unethical only if it is successful? This resonates with the long-scrutinised tussle in the epic story of the *Mahabharata* between assessing an action on the basis of moral duties or consequences.[2]

Standards of right and wrong in financial markets need to be far higher than elsewhere and higher than the law can reasonably provide for a couple of reasons. There are two features of retail markets, especially in food and drink, that make them examples of markets that function well. First it is easy and quick to assess quality; second there is frequent repeat business, which reveals consumers' judgements on quality. In such a market, suppliers have very strong incentives to keep standards high. When you buy a bad apple at a supermarket in London three times in a row, you stop buying apples there. If it happens to enough people, the supermarket soon gets the message and changes its supplier. It cannot rest on its laurels, as many consumer brands like Marks & Spencer have discovered over the years.

Major financial decisions are not made weekly. They are made infrequently. Most people make a decision on their pension only twice: when they join and when they leave. The time it takes to realise you have made a mistake with your pension, mortgage or car loan means it is often too late to do much about it. So, unlike supermarkets, it is harder for the financial markets to root out bad apples. These problems have suggested certain solutions. For example, improving disclosure of information to make it easier for people to arrive at the right decision is a key requirement of financial regulation today. Another solution is the development of products and rules that allow people to chop and change their financial suppliers more easily, be it banks, insurers, mortgage providers or pension advisers. Witness the development of "portable pensions" and innovations that allow individuals to "opt out" of state benefits. Disclosure and flexibility are the main weapons of our financial regulators today.

However, these solutions are about trying to ameliorate the problems, not tackling them head-on. The distinction is important because the inherent problem may not, in fact, be very reducible at all. When past performance is no guide to the future, it is not clear that having disclosure standards is going to provide better decision-making processes. It may well be that the outcome of financial decisions that involve ordinary folk investing for the future, or borrowing against their future, will always be unclear for a long while. By the time it is clear whether the right decision was taken or not, the person or institution who sold you the product may be nowhere to be found. The degree of uncertainty and time-scale involved means that the unscrupulous players can survive for long, undermining the more scrupulous. Where there is little distinction between the good and bad advisers, except in the long run, Gresham's law will apply, and the bad financial agents will drive out the good. The legislators response has been to provide guarantees, explicit or otherwise, but that creates a moral hazard as it encourages institutions to take more risks under the security of the guarantee, and so the legislators end up promoting even more regulation.

Transparency is generally good, but it is not the answer to every ailment and can sometimes be inappropriate. In the case of disclosing past returns, it may give a misleading impression. In some cases it can lead to poor behaviour such as an unwillingness to invest in the necessary research, or an incentive to take advantage of someone else's position. The bottom line is that finance depends on trust and in financial transactions mere laws, rules and information alone cannot achieve trust. We need ethical behaviour.

■ Short-selling

One area in which the transparency debate rages is in the case of short-selling: where investors sell more of a stock (or other financial instrument) than they own, in the expectation that they will be able to buy the stock at a cheaper price later. Recently it has been alleged that on many occasions, short-sellers sell the stock of a company to the point where covenants with its banks or bond holders are triggered, which requires the company to take some action (such as a new issue of shares, fire-sale of assets or liquidation of stocks) that will validate the new lower price of the shares. The late Kenneth Lay, former chairman of Enron, believed that his company was "brought down", not by unethical practices at Enron, but by the unethical behaviour of short-sellers. Many insurance companies which earn an extra premium by lending stocks to others, have voiced concern, with some degree of moral indignation, that they do not wish to lend them to short-sellers. Short-selling is not illegal, is it unethical?

The distinction we would draw is not between "overselling" or buying stocks. The more symmetrical these activities are, the more efficient markets will be. The distinction is whether the short-seller is selling the stock because her view is that it is overvalued and she wants to get ahead of a decline in the share price that may otherwise occur without her trade, or whether she is selling the stock as part of a contrivance that is designed to bring the stock lower in a manner that would not have occurred were she not to short the stock. There are parallels between the ethics of this behaviour and the Citibank government bond trade that are touched on elsewhere in this chapter.

● Case study:
CITIGROUP AND MTS

Of all the world's top financial institutions none has aspired to do more than Citigroup under Chuck Prince's leadership to address ethical problems and attempt to instil an ethical culture. Citigroup has nonetheless suffered high-profile ethical lapses in its operations around the world. The story of how this giant institution confronted its problems is worth telling because it shows just how difficult it can be to instil sound values throughout a diverse and complex international organisation.

When Chuck Prince became CEO in 2003 Citigroup was under pressure from regulators and suffering severe reputational damage that threatened to tarnish its brand. It had been a prominent provider of finance, on and off-balance sheet, to Enron, WorldCom, Adelphia and Parmalat, among others. The publicity attaching to these scandals was woeful and it was not helped by some very maladroit behaviour by bonus-hungry bankers. A prime example related to Citigroup's role in helping remove liabilities from the Parmalat balance sheet through a vehicle the bank's executives chose to call Buco Nero – Italian for Black Hole. When this came out after Parmalat's bankruptcy it was widely seen as symptomatic of a cynical and opportunistic culture aimed at maximising Citigroup's short-term profits regardless of ethical considerations.

Apart from damaging the bank's brand these relationships with companies that turned out to be fraudulent proved expensive. In 2004, without admitting any wrongdoing, Citigroup settled a lawsuit with disgruntled WorldCom shareholders for $2.6 billion while putting aside a further $6.6 billion against the potential cost of other scandals.

ENTER A NEW BROOM

Chuck Prince, who had been general counsel to CEO Sandy Weill, recognised when he succeeded Weill as CEO in 2003 that the leadership task required more attention to business ethics. In its 2003 annual report the financial giant declared: "We aspire to be known as a company with the highest standards of moral and ethical conduct – working to earn client trust, day in and day out. Our word is our bond." Other aspirations included being customer-centred and "an organisation people can trust". In a jointly authored statement, Chuck Prince and Bob Willumstad, the president, said:

Importantly, in 2003 we continued our thorough re-examination of the way we do business, with an eye toward developing standards that are not merely 'common industry practice' or 'letter of the law' but the best practices in a given area. We need to be clear about this subject: because of our size and scope, because of the benefits of our position of business leadership, we are held to a higher standard. We accept this responsibility. We created Business Practice committees in each of our core businesses to foster a candid exchange of information and to reinforce the most important discipline across our company: to always act in a way that earns the trust of our customers and the respect of our regulators. This is a permanent effort, a process now embedded in our business and our culture so that Citigroup is always reaching to set the very highest standards.

This was all very admirable. But the high aspiration was also a hostage to fortune; for, in 2004 Citigroup was obliged to acknowledge that it had reputational problems in Japan and Europe. Our main focus here is on the London operations, which were mired in controversy over a trade in the European sovereign bond market that raised important ethical issues.

In July 2004 the European government bond desk at the bank's Citigroup Global Capital Markets Limited (CGML) subsidiary was encouraged to increase profits from proprietary trading and the development of new trading strategies. In pursuit of this the bank's traders planned a move that came to be known as the "Dr Evil" trade. It was designed to exploit a weakness in the structure of the Italian-based MTS electronic bond market, or the Società per il Mercato dei Titoli di Stato, to give it its full title. This market, developed by banks in cooperation with European governments to enhance the tradeability of European sovereign debt, required market makers to commit themselves to quote prices for bonds for at least five hours a day for certain minimum amounts. In the normal course of events a market maker would expect to be dealing in up to ten different bonds.

Citigroup's traders realised that this commitment to deal left its market making competitors vulnerable. So they proposed that the desk create a trade in the cash bond market and in the futures market to exploit this weakness.

On a quiet Monday in August 2004 the trading desk swung into action on both the cash and the futures markets. At the heart of this trade, initiated at 10.28 a.m., was a transaction that involved the placing of sell orders worth €11.3 billion in 18 seconds on the MTS market, which was equivalent to a full average day's trading volume on MTS. It also sold around €1.5 billion on other domestic cash markets resulting in a total sale of no less than 200 different bonds worth nearly €13 billion. Then at 11.25 a.m. it bought bonds on MTS at a lower price, closing part of its short position at a profit. Because of their commitment to deal, or provide liquidity, in the jargon, Citigroup's competitors were hit as the big bank cleared a substantial profit on the deal. Competitors were stung for losses of €1–2 million apiece.

To prevent a repetition MTS felt obliged to restrict trading, while some banks refused to honour their commitment to make a market in case they were hit by another mass order. The resulting decline in market liquidity caused finance ministries around Europe to start worrying about the possibility that the cost of servicing their government's debt would rise, since investors expect to be compensated for a decline in liquidity by higher interest rates. In the event, trading volume on the MTS market declined by more than 30 per cent in the three months following the Dr Evil trade, though how far the Citigroup trade contributed to this loss of revenue is impossible to quantify. And as the furore over the deal mounted, regulators across Europe started to look into the transaction.

TWO VIEWS OF THE TRADE

From an ethical point of view, some outside Citigroup as well as within took the view that this was a market used by professional traders who knew how to look after themselves and that exploiting a structural weakness in the MTS system was fair game. The controversial trade might even have been beneficial if it speeded up reform of what many regarded as a flawed trading system. Others felt that the market worked on the basis of a gentleman's agreement which Citigroup had cynically breached. What is clear, though, is that Citigroup's traders were flouting the bank's declared values and behaving in a way that was scarcely customer-centred or in tune with the aspiration to be an organisation that people could trust. In no way were they living up to the commitment by the people at the top to observe the highest ethical standards.

From a business perspective the trade was a disaster. European governments, and especially the Italian government, which according to one insider was Citigroup's most important European fixed interest client, were angry. The bank lost governmental business. And the regulatory backlash was harsh. Britain's Financial Services Authority imposed a fine of £14m for a failure to exercise due skill, care and diligence, together with failures of internal control and risk management, although it also concluded that Citigroup had not deliberately set out to disrupt or distort the market. This was the highest fine ever meted out to a bank in London. An investigation conducted by MTS's own appeals board in response to its complaint against Citigroup was highly critical, accusing the bank of violating a number of the regulations governing conduct in the MTS market. Its Wise Men Committee of independent outsiders, whose role was to adjudicate on any allegations of breach of the MTS market's regulations, concluded the following: Citigroup had prejudiced the smooth operation of the market in the long run as well as in its short-run impact; the bank had manifested a lack of professionalism in its evident disregard of how the trade would affect the market; the trade was not executed with adequate professionalism and diligence; the traders had no training that dealt with the MTS regulations and inadequate knowledge of the interface between their in-house computer system and the MTS electronic market.

In fact the report of the Committee of Wise Men, which we have seen, suggests that the failure to test the software used for the trade almost resulted in a fiasco. Immediately after the button was pushed to launch the trade, the traders themselves were puzzled as to the outcome. This led them to panic and to push the button a second time, causing Citigroup to make additional sales of bonds so that its short position was substantially increased and the risks in the trade greatly expanded. It also appears that the profits earned from buying back the bonds were far greater, in consequence, than anyone had expected. "All this is evidence", the Wise Men Committee concluded, "of a serious lack of professionalism and diligence in the execution of what was a highly risky trade of unprecedented size." As a result Citigroup was suspended from trading on the MTS system for a month in 2005.

KNUCKLEHEADS KEEP THEIR JOBS

The purpose of this narrative is not primarily to explore the morality or otherwise of the controversial trade, in which those involved were manifestly not concerned about the consequences of their actions for Citigroup's clients or the integrity of the MTS market. Rather, it is to consider the response of the people at the top of the bank and look at the difficulties of instilling values throughout a large organisation. In the first instance, the response of CEO Chuck Prince was to call the trade "knuckleheaded". The traders were suspended. Then a contrite email sent to employees by Tom Maheras, Citigroup's head of global capital markets, was leaked to the press, stating "we did not meet our standards in this instance and, as a result, we regret having executed this transaction".

Citigroup is committed to holding itself to the highest standards in its business practices," he added. "Unfortunately, we failed to fully consider [the transaction's] impact on our clients, other market participants and our regulators.

Yet in due course the traders returned to work and there was no news of anyone being fired for an act that had severely damaged the bank's reputation, brand and underlying business. We suspect the profits on the trade were insufficient to compensate for the loss of governmental mandates suffered by Citigroup in the wake of the fiasco. And the morale of employees who did believe in the values trumpeted by top executives was undermined. For, as it was put to us by one of the bank's employees, who understandably wished to remain anonymous, "not to fire these bond traders or their management is to internally celebrate their doings and it has led to an uncomfortable vacuum about what values the organisation believes in and what the strategy is".

The failure to fire anyone was doubly inexplicable because Citigroup showed itself willing, that year, to fire three of its highest ranking executives after the Japanese Financial Services Agency ordered the closure of Citigroup's private bank in Japan in the light of regulatory breaches that the watchdog said had allowed large profits to be amassed illegally. Chuck Prince was obliged to apologise to the Japanese, while admitting that senior staff had put short term profits ahead of the bank's long-term reputation – which was precisely what the traders in London had done. In discussing the controversial trade with senior Citigroup executives we have been unable to establish why no one was immediately fired, beyond being told that employment law considerations were part of the explanation. But whatever the reasons, the practical outcome was that Citigroup's leaders ended up sending a contradictory signal to the group's employees, while opening themselves to the charge of hypocrisy for failing to respond adequately to such a flagrant breach of Citigroup's declared values and code of conduct. Citigroup's top executives had, after all, told all the employees in April 2004:

"We live by our values and expect all who work for us to live by them as well. They are vital to securing and maintaining respect from our shareholders, employees, government officials and the public at large. They are central to our business franchise."

In the light of Citigroup's response to the notorious trade, any dispassionate observer would surely be entitled to wonder about the likely efficacy of Chuck Prince's subsequent extensive efforts to engage in a dialogue on Citigroup's values with employees and implement a five-point plan to inspire and monitor good behaviour. It is hard to escape the conclusion that there was inconsistency in Chuck Prince's efforts to implement an ethical programme in this giant organisation, given that he showed he could act decisively when Citigroup's reputation was at risk by firing top executives over violations of the law in Japan. This points to a fundamental lesson. If top management fails to respond adequately to flagrant breaches of the organisation's values, the ethical task risks being subverted from the outset.

● Case study:
TALISMAN ENERGY

Talisman is the largest Canadian-based independent oil and natural gas producer, with operations in Canada, the North Sea, Indonesia and, until recently, Sudan. A former subsidiary of BP, it is now a widely held company listed in Canada on the Toronto stock exchange and in the United States on the New York stock exchange. Talisman is included in the TSE 35 and the S&P/TSE 60 indices, so investors in these indices would end up with an automatic stake in Talisman. This case study discusses the ethical considerations of Talisman as an investor in a pipeline in Sudan and the ethical considerations of investors in Talisman.

Talisman acquired an interest in the Greater Nile Petroleum Operating Company (GNPOC), a joint oil and pipeline development in southern Sudan, when it purchased Arakis Energy of Calgary in 1998. GNPOC was owned by Talisman Energy of Calgary (25%), China National Petroleum Corporation (40%), Malaysia's Petronas Carigali (30%) and Sudan's Sudapet (5%).

From Talisman's perspective, its partners in the GNPOC were strategic industry investors, experienced and long-term players – good partners with which to try to monetise oil resources in a challenging environment. But for many human rights activists and some shareholders, this was a joint venture between companies with poor human rights records, operating in a country fraught with human rights issues. Apart from the poverty of many of Sudan's inhabitants, worsened by a challenging climate, Sudan was ravaged by civil war. Indeed, there is a raging debate today as to whether what went on in Darfur, in Sudan, could be classified as genocide, supported by the military. But whether it is genocide or not, the conflict has exacted a heavy toll. Out of a population of 40 million, nearly 2 million people died between 1983 and 2005 as a result of the conflict. In excess of

4 million people are internally displaced, dispossessed of their homes and separated from their families.

It is alleged by many that the development of oil is intensifying the conflict in Sudan. (In the authors' experience, in most countries oil proves to be a poison to economic development and it is best lost, not found.) Oil revenue to the government of Sudan is estimated at $300 million to $500 million annually. Military spending has increased significantly since GNPOC's operations began. According to one shareholder activist, "The African state of Sudan has been embroiled in civil war for most of its forty-four years of independence. The role of oil and the centrality of the dispute over resources is now emerging as one of the most important factors in this devastating crisis; and Talisman Energy Inc., a Canadian oil company, is in the middle of it." [3]

Amnesty International, Human Rights Watch, two United Nations Special Rapporteurs and the Canadian government-commissioned Harker Report, all provided substantial documentation of human rights abuses, and these were not of a mild variety. These groups cite slavery, forced displacement, torture and rape. Human rights organisations argue that the oil revenues from the GNPOC are being used by the government to subsidise (encourage) and intensify these atrocities. According to the Harker Report, the fact-finding mission commissioned by Canada in November of 1999:

We can only conclude that Sudan is a place of extraordinary suffering and continuing human rights violations, even though some forward progress can be recorded, and the oil operations in which a Canadian company [Talisman] is involved add more suffering (page 16). Talisman Energy Inc.'s involvement in GNPOC is supporting the Government of Sudan regime, both through resources, as well as providing moral cover. Talisman's 'constructive engagement' in Sudan does not work.

Talisman's response was that it had witnessed no human rights violations associated with its project in Sudan and that it upholds ethical standards in its operations. The company suggested that the prosperity brought by oil development could help advance peace, and welcomed Canada's decision not to impose economic sanctions against Sudan.

Initially investor groups asked that the company take steps to ensure that revenues which were received by the Sudanese government from Talisman's involvement in the Greater Nile project were not being used to finance the government's war efforts. This would involve a degree of intervention in the government of Sudan that is not ordinarily feasible or justifiable and so some investor activists argued that if the company could not reassure investors that revenues from the pipeline were not associated with human rights abuses the company should pull out of the operation until such assurance was available.

Talisman could have argued that it was by no means clear how its disinvestment would make matters better and they could see how it could make matters worse for the employees of the pipeline and all the other worthwhile activities that were funded by it. They responded by adopting the International Code of Ethics for Canadian Business. But shareholder activists were unimpressed by this, as the code provides no specific standards or prescribed process for implementation, monitoring or reporting.

In addition to the perceived risk of human rights abuse, shareholders filing resolutions expressing concern over Talisman's activities in Sudan raised the very real spectre of declining share value. They asserted that without credible evidence to show that Talisman is not contributing to continuing civil war or gross and systematic human rights abuses in Sudan, the company's long-term financial health may be adversely affected. This factor weighed on the company's management and, after a long fight, Talisman decided to sell its equity stake in a private sale to Indian-based ONGC Videsh.

CORPORATE SOCIAL RESPONSIBILITY

Talisman argued that it was being a good corporate citizen: investing in a poor country and doing so in accordance with an international code of good investment behaviour. It is not alone in trying to convince consumers, shareholders and others that they are being good corporate citizens. In recent years Corporate Social Responsibility (CSR) has been a growth business. There is a tension between those who view CSR as an attempt by companies to apply benchmarks in trying to do good and those who view it as an attempt to bolster their PR by appearing to do good. These are not mutually exclusive of course. A cynic would point to the fact that many codes appear anodyne, subjective and hard to measure and that those companies who operate in the most environmentally and socially sensitive sectors and need the most PR, such as the extraction industries, are the biggest contributors to CSR programmes. However, it is also the case that there are many examples of companies and investors being good corporate citizens – establishing AIDS clinics or supporting environmental campaigns for example – whether they do so through a code or not.

In modern society companies need virtual "licences to operate" based on their social and environmental impact. These are not actual, formal, licences, but tacit permission that can be removed through legislation, or a consumers' or investors' strike if a company behaves poorly. After Enron, this permission was removed in the case of Andersen, the accounting firm, and it collapsed, despite a previously robust business model, amid deserting customers and legal actions. Barclays Bank might have suffered the same fate had it not pulled out of apartheid South Africa. It is what led Talisman to pull out of Sudan. Monopolies are particularly sensitive to losing their tacit or real permission to operate, which is why they are big spenders on CSR-related activities. Ever wondered why EdF, a French-based electricity company with regional electricity franchises in the UK, sponsors English football? If companies are investing in doing good to preserve their permission to operate, CSR codes could play a useful role in focusing their energies and provide some priorities and standards for the many diverse initiatives. Therefore, while we believe CSR is no substitute for creating an environment in which a company gives serious consideration to ethical issues, CSR may be part of a legitimate process of highlighting ethical responsibilities and priorities for companies and investors in those companies.

AN ETHICAL FRAMEWORK FOR SPECULATORS

The questions set out at the end of the chapter are intended to help us all to evaluate better our ethical position. We do not expect the answers to be simple.

We present this ethical guide for speculators with three objectives in mind. One aim is higher ethical standards that lead to a more inclusive financial system. Another is that while being more mindful of morality, standards are not to be imposed upon people in suffocating ways. One of the strengths of a liberal economy is that individuals have choices and so long as laws set out our basic standards, individuals and business should be free to make their own, higher, moral choices in pursuing their corporate social responsibility. Of course, choice and responsibility are not easy. Many of us would rather some choices were taken from us. The third objective is to keep our ethical guide simple to use and focused. While there is an increasing emphasis on ethical standards, they are not always meaningfully defined. At every corner is a company adopting an ethical code. But many of these codes are empty. They tend to have just three elements: a call to be ethical (where ethics are not defined), a requirement to obey the law and a warning against having a conflict of interest with the firm.

There is an alternative. In the course of observing many financial decisions, we have often seen market participants hesitate before deciding whether to go ahead with a transaction. In the *Zeitgeist*, you may describe it as a "Kouros moment", when they briefly assess whether the transaction makes sense or, as Daniel Hodson, former chairman of LIFFE would say, "smells funny". In that moment, they usually ask themselves whether they know individuals involved and whether such a transaction has been done before. Neither question proposes a very exacting ethical standard – especially in a market where there is kudos for the new. This book tries to provide market participants with a few more questions that they should ask themselves. But it is up to individual investors how they behave. Indeed, a key message for us is that responsibilities are not with the companies or codes they have signed up to, but with individuals.

As we have noted elsewhere, our questions centre around three issues – disguise, contrivance and harm – but our starting point is to make sure that we have not devolved our ethical responsibility to someone else or something else. In the case of Talisman or any other investor, signing up to the International Code of Ethics for Canadian Business should not in any way have made the company feel that this had shifted ethical responsibility to those who authored the code. They remained responsible for the appropriateness and relevance of the code, for uncodified unethical activities or issues of the effectiveness, enforcement and monitoring of the code.

The principal ethical concern for Talisman and investors in Talisman is whether their investment was causing or abetting in unmitigated harm to the people of Sudan. Questions are easier to pose than answers. Many would say there is no question that the company was abetting a sordid scene. Others may ask what would be different if Talisman were not a shareholder of the GNPOC? Into this grey area could be added whether the company was doing enough to mitigate any harm that may have been caused indirectly from its involvement in the pipeline. The point of our book is not to dictate a solution, but to make individuals ask themselves these questions and to act only when they are satisfied with the answers. The more questions are asked and the more actions need to be justified, the more likely it is that we end up in a better place. Avoiding unmitigated harm is not the only ethical issue for investors. One of our key concerns for all market participants, including investors, is that there should be no disguised and unmanaged conflicts of interest. These are prevalent in finance, but not clearly so in the case of Talisman's investments in Sudan or Citigroup's bond trade. Another major concern is being party to contrivances that serve to put some party at a disadvantage. Perhaps there were issues attached to how Talisman ended up with its 25 per cent stake or on what basis it sold the stake to ONGC Videsh, but on the face of it this was a straightforward transaction. Contrivance of course was at the heart of the ethical concern over the Citigroup trade and our concerns over some short-selling activities. The point of these trading strategies was to create an artificial situation where the trader could buy back instruments from counterparties at a lower price than they had previously sold them and at a lower price than they would otherwise have been able to buy them.

The public trading markets are particularly prone to rogue players, who can undermine confidence in the industry and thus the economy. At the end of the day, corporate ethics officers aside, individuals need to make their own moral choices. We do not think these can be easily codified into a list of dos and don'ts and we make no attempt to present such a list. What we do believe is that people can be helped to make ethical choices by helping them to reflect on their actions by asking themselves the appropriate questions.

➤ QUESTIONS INVESTORS AND SPECULATORS SHOULD ASK THEMSELVES

1. Am I trying to devolve my ethical responsibilities to someone else like the company management, government or writers of codes of good investment conduct?

2. As an investor, am I causing or abetting unmitigated harm to any of the stakeholders or the marketplace, if I carry out this investment?

3. Are there any disguised or unmanaged conflicts than influence how I will buy or sell my investment?

4. Is my investment return a result of any contrived circumstances or strategies that have put some party at a disadvantage? Would a comparable investment return be available to someone else who did not employ my strategy?

NOTES:

1 Laura Nyantung Beny, Do Insider Trading Laws Matter? Some Preliminary Comparative Evidence, *American Law and Economics Review* 7: 1 (Oxford UP, 2005) 144-83.

2 The Mahabharata is an epic story that dates back to the 6th and 8th century BC. It tells of events that are supposed to have taken place around the 12th century BC. According to the Mahabharata, Arjuna, a master archer, was reluctant to take part in the battle because the slaughter he knew he would cause in the enemy ranks. He was persuaded by his charioteer, Lord Krishna, to change his mind. Their philosophical discourse is about the issues involved in war – courage, a warrior's duty and the nature of human life.

3 The Harker Report on Sudan was prepared by diplomat John Harker for the Canadian Foreign Affairs Minister. It was released in November 2000 by the Canadian Department of Foreign Affairs.

Chapter 6

CREATIVE ACCOUNTING/ HITTING THE NUMBERS

SPEED-READ SUMMARY

- The credibility of top executives in the Anglo-American model of capitalism depends on their generating consistent increases in earnings and carefully guiding analysts' expectations.

- With performance criteria for bonuses and share incentive schemes increasingly linked to the share price, the temptation to massage earnings numbers is acute.

- Partly thanks to aggressive earnings management, US corporate profits were significantly overstated in the late 1990s, sending misleading signals to the markets and resulting in the misallocation of capital.

- Massaging the numbers can be done legitimately, but the ethical question is often one of degree: is it just a way of reducing short-term share price volatility, or is it more seriously misleading in a way that could ultimately damage the company and destroy shareholder value? There is evidence that managers are increasingly prepared to destroy value in the interests of smoothing earnings.

- A key question concerns motivation. Managers may be tempted to keep shareholders in the dark to preserve their jobs or to give a boost to the share price to help inflate bonuses or equity-related incentive scheme awards.

In the Anglo-American model of capitalism, the stock market imposes a ferocious discipline on the managers of quoted companies. For a start, the movement of the company share price offers a minute-by-minute critical commentary on corporate performance and prospects. Quarterly results are closely examined by stock market analysts, professional fund managers and business journalists, and there is an ever-present threat of hostile takeover. The credibility of top executives in this system depends on their generating consistent increases in earnings. They also have to develop the art of carefully guiding analysts' expectations and subsequently "hitting the numbers". Any shortfall of performance against expectation can result in a sickening slide in the share price and an immediate question being raised over the tenure of the chief executive and chief financial officer.

CEOs UNDER PRESSURE

Putting CEOs into a financial pressure cooker in this way has its disadvantages. The underlying assumption is that companies are capable of delivering consistently rising, above-average earnings. Yet this is absurd because all companies cannot be above average. Equally absurd is the implicit assumption that accountancy is a precise, objective science capable of producing a single exact number that is worth hitting. The reality is that in the modern knowledge economy, accountancy is more a matter of judgement than ever before. The system also creates a tension between short-term earnings performance and long-term value creation. As for the discipline, it is peculiar in that top executives set the benchmarks against which they themselves are measured. It is as if pupils were shown the answers to the mathematics exam the evening before and then thrown out of school if they failed to achieve full marks on the day. The discipline is nonetheless real and top executives do fail for one reason or another to meet their own benchmarks. And the US capital market approach is being adopted increasingly by other countries around the world despite the questionable definition of performance.

Because so many employees now own stock in the company where they work, the categorical imperative of hitting the numbers may be felt throughout the organisation. Inevitably there is a temptation, in this ritualised expectations game, to massage the results to keep the stock price up. Where performance criteria for bonuses and stock incentive schemes are related to the behaviour of the stock, the temptation is particularly acute. In the wave of corporate scandals from Enron to Royal Dutch Shell, this pressure drove top executives to cook the books, which had the effect of boosting their own compensation packages. Yet it is also open to executives to tailor quite lawfully their spending decisions and choice of accounting policies in order to smooth the quarterly earnings trend.

KIDDER PEABODY DISASTER

The nature of these dilemmas emerges in a surprising way in the autobiography of Jack Welch, former chairman and CEO of General Electric, most notably when he recounts the disaster that struck the big conglomerate's investment banking subsidiary, Kidder Peabody, in 1994. Kidder's government bond trading desk was run by Joseph Jett, who made a series of fictitious trades to inflate his own bonus. These artificial trades had inflated Kidder's reported income and the team of GE managers that was sent in to assess the damage concluded, with GE's first quarter earnings release due to be published in just two days' time, that a $350 million write-off would be needed to deal with the financial black hole left by the rogue trader.

Welch explains how he apologised to 14 of GE's business leaders for what had happened and felt terrible because this nightmarish surprise would hit the stock and hurt every GE employee. And he continues:

The response of our business leaders to the crisis was typical of the GE culture. Even though the books had closed on the quarter, many immediately offered to pitch in to cover the Kidder gap. Some said they could find an extra $10 million, $20 million, and even $30 million from their businesses to offset the surprise. Though it was too late, their willingness to help was a dramatic contrast to the excuses I had been hearing from the Kidder people.

Instead of pitching in, they complained about how this disaster was going to affect their incomes. 'This is going to ruin everything,' one said. 'Our bonus is down the toilet. How will we keep anyone?' The two cultures and their differences never stood out so clearly in my mind. All I heard was, 'I didn't do it. I never saw it. I never met with him. I didn't talk to him.' No one seemed to know anyone or work for anyone.

It was disgusting.[1]

For Jack Welch the ethical issue here boils down to the contrast between the selfish, footloose individualism embedded in the culture of Wall Street's investment banks and the healthy team spirit exemplified by managers in GE's mainstream businesses. He seems astonishingly blind to the possibility that others might be shocked that the corporate culture at GE was one in which offering to play fast and loose with the quarterly numbers was regarded as good teamwork. Some might argue that on the Richter scale of ethical lapses this does not rate very high. Apologists could no doubt claim that smoothing the numbers is an antidote to stock market short-termism and thus in the interests of all shareholders. The fact that the market responds so fiercely to missed earnings targets suggests that investors anyway believe that most companies can "find the money" to meet targets and that missing a target is an indication of very poor management.

Yet while it is true that smoothing quarterly earnings is a rational response to the somewhat arbitrary discipline of the capital market expectations game, there is also a question about whether shareholders should have been told on what basis this was being done at GE, not least because such an opaque approach to reporting can put management on to a slippery slope. For the risk, in creative accounting, is that managers end up fooling themselves about the real profitability and viability of the businesses they run.

PROFITS ADJUSTED DOWNWARDS

That, indeed, is what appears to have happened across much of the US corporate sector in the 1990s. Revisions to the official estimates of US corporate profits have shown that American corporations were far less profitable in the second half of the

1990s than was thought at the time. Research by economists at the Federal Reserve Bank of New York has shown that the downward adjustments to the official corporate profit numbers at that time were among the largest revisions of the past 40 years and represented a sharp reversal of the previous trend of upward revisions.[2] The economists found a marked disparity between the profits recorded in the financial accounts of companies and the profits as portrayed in the country's National Income and Product Accounts. And a study by the US General Accounting Office found that the number of earnings restatements filed with the Securities and Exchange Commission in the second half of the 1990s increased dramatically.[3] Such filings are required where companies have significantly misreported their profits.

Part of the explanation lies in the increase in the use of stock options. Because US business leaders successfully lobbied to persuade the accountancy profession to drop a proposal to expense stock options in the profit and loss account, this employment cost was not charged against the profits disclosed in the financial accounts. So it proved difficult for official statisticians to make sound estimates at the time for the national accounts, in which stock option awards are treated as a cost and deducted from profits. Revisions were then made on the basis of tax accounts submitted later by companies to the tax authorities. Academics have calculated that stock options may account for half the difference between tax and financial income in the 1990s.

AGGRESSIVE ACCOUNTING

Yet it is also likely that aggressive accounting played a part in conveying the exaggerated impression of profits. The General Accounting Office's work, supported by academic research that comes to similar conclusions,[4] shows that companies were particularly aggressive in the second half of the 1990s in recognising revenues earlier than permitted by generally accepted accounting principles. And we know that WorldCom and Qwest alone, in the telecommunications sector, overstated earnings for 1999 and 2000 by around $4 billion. As a result of the investigative efforts of Eliot Spitzer, New York State Attorney General, we also know that American International Group overstated earnings by using reinsurance contracts that lacked commercial substance and helped window dress the giant insurance company's balance sheet. A final possibility is that the growth in use of aggressive tax shelters may explain the discrepancies between financial accounts and tax accounts.[5]

All of this matters because corporate profits play an important part in establishing the attractiveness or otherwise of business expenditure on capital investment, research and development and employee development. Profits also provide an important signal to the markets. It seems all too clear that the overstatement of corporate profits in the 1990s resulted in investors and corporate managers misallocating capital. So by fooling themselves as to the profitability of their own companies, managers were inflicting a cost on the wider economy.

DIFFERENT KINDS OF SMOOTHING

From an ethical perspective it is important to distinguish between different kinds of smoothing. In any given financial year, most companies face choices of accounting principles, which can lead to differing profit outcomes. Given the expectations of the capital markets, few would blame a management that opted for a legitimate accounting policy that delivered a number more likely to satisfy the markets. Yet there is also a question of degree. Choices that constantly and consistently paint a relentlessly optimistic picture of the state of the business can end up misleading shareholders. National attitudes vary around the world on whether this is ethically dubious. In the US, for example, taking accountancy to the limits of legality is regarded with a less jaundiced eye than in the UK. In a US class action against the British telecoms company Cable & Wireless, a judge in Virginia even referred to non-disclosure of a contingent liability in the accounts as "legitimate business puffery".[6]

Then there is the separate issue of earnings manipulation that involves economic actions taken by the management to help meet market expectations. Profits can very easily be raised, for example, by deferring decisions on current and capital expenditure, including expenditure in such important and sensitive areas as health and safety. And there is some evidence that since the introduction of the Sarbanes-Oxley Act in 2002, US executives are more hesitant to take risks with accountancy and more inclined to smooth earnings through real actions. A Duke University and University of Washington study of more than 400 senior financial executives found in 2004 that 78 per cent were willing to sacrifice shareholder value to smooth earnings. Some 80 per cent said they would decrease discretionary spending on research and development or advertising and maintenance to meet an earnings target, while 55 per cent said they would not embark on an obviously profitable project if it would cause them to miss the consensus earnings target in the current quarter.[7]

This is an amazing comment on the capital market expectations game. At first sight it appears outrageous that executives are willing to destroy economic value simply to meet market expectations. Given that the findings are freely admitted, it also raises questions about what else is going on that has not been freely vouchsafed to the authors of the study. Yet as the authors make clear, most of those involved saw this form of value destruction as the lesser of two evils, because the stock market response to a missed target could lead to a loss of shareholder value as well as reputational loss for the executives concerned. What this suggests is that there is, in effect, a Faustian compact. The markets believe well-managed companies can always find a way of meeting the targets; and because executives know that missing a target will be perceived as a dreadful commentary on management's ability and may point to deep-seated problems, they will move heaven and earth to find the numbers to pre-empt the havoc that would otherwise be wreaked on the share price.

As with difficult judgements about choices of accounting policy, there is a question of degree. How long do you continue destroying value before throwing in the towel on the share price? A more fundamental question arises where compensation is geared to earnings or affected by the level of the share price. Outside shareholders would be entitled to ask whether the perceived lesser of two evils concerns the individual executive's personal financial position or a wider criterion of shareholder value.

QUESTIONS TO BE ASKED

All of this gives rise to an important issue about how far aggressive earnings manipulation is compatible with prudent management. Yet that in no way diminishes the fact that there is also an ethical issue, which concerns the extent to which management misleads shareholders. This is the sort of grey area where it is hard to make satisfactory generalisations. It is nonetheless possible to highlight questions executives should ask in relation to smoothing the numbers. The most basic one concerns failure to be open with shareholders about earnings manipulation. Is it really in the shareholders' interest for the short-term earnings trend to be smoothed without making clear that this is happening? Or is it simply convenient for managers to keep shareholders in the dark as a means of preserving their own jobs? Is there a risk that the short-term benefit to the share price of massaging earnings will be outweighed by longer-term adverse consequences? Or, more crudely, are earnings being relentlessly massaged against a background of deteriorating corporate performance in the hope that something will turn up? Has the degree of aggression in massaging earnings been influenced by earnings-related incentive arrangements and bonuses for managers?

Openness in business is usually a good principle, except where it would inflict competitive disadvantage on the company concerned. And this applies particularly in areas where the principal/agent conflict arises. So in the context of earnings manipulation, a very basic principle would be that management should "tell it like it is" unless openness would demonstrably inflict damage on shareholders or other stakeholders. That said, it has to be acknowledged that the capital market expectations game is a flawed form of accountability. It reduces the relationship between managers and shareholders, and the analysis of corporate performance, to an oversimplified credibility test. So the wider question for all the participants is whether to play at all. In the US, Coca-Cola has led the way in refusing to offer guidance on quarterly earnings.

What is also required to make the system work better is for fund managers to take a more strategic view and recognise the limitations of quarterly reporting. Their difficulty is that their time horizons are heavily influenced by yet another financial discipline – that of quarterly or even monthly assessments of investment performance in a very competitive market for fund management mandates. It follows that the US capital market model will continue to pose a business challenge and an ethical test for all the participants in a systemically flawed game.

➤ QUESTIONS FOR DIRECTORS AND FINANCIAL MANAGERS

1. Is it really in the shareholders' interest for the short-term earnings trend to be smoothed?

2. Are you sure you are not keeping shareholders in the dark primarily as a means of preserving your job or inflating bonuses or other equity-related awards?

3. How great is the risk that the short-term benefit to the share price of massaging earnings will be outweighed by longer-term adverse consequences? Do you think the short-term/long-term trade-off is one that shareholders would consider justified if they were subsequently to find out?

4. Are you sure you are not on a slippery slope – is it ethical to continue massaging the numbers, when corporate performance is deteriorating, in the hope that something will turn up?

5. Would it not be better to provide guidance to the analysts about the temporary nature of an earnings blip where it is caused by necessary investment, rather than cutting investment to boost the short-term earnings figure?

6. Is the "hitting the numbers" culture in the company so endemic that it could blind you to the possibility that your aggressive accounting may be unethical?

NOTES

1   *Jack Straight from the Gut*, by Jack Welch with John A. Byrne (Warner Books, 2001).

2   Recent Revisions to Corporate Profits: What We Know and When We Knew It, by Charles P. Himmelberg, James M. Mahoney, April Bang and Brian Chernoff, *Current Issues in Economics and Finance*, 10: 3 (Federal Reserve Bank of New York, March 2004).

3   *Financial Statement Restatements: Trends, Market Impacts, Regulatory Responses, and Remaining Challenges*. Report to the Chairman, Senate Committee on Banking, Housing, and Urban Affairs. GAO-03-138 (October 2002).

4   *Trends in Book-Tax Income and Balance Sheet Differences*, by Lillian F. Mills, Kaye J. Newberry and William B. Trautman, Social Science Research Network, Working Paper Series (2002).

5   Quantitative Measures of the Quality of Financial Reporting, George B. Moriarty and Philip B. Livingston. *Financial Executive* (July/August 2001).

6   See *The Corporate Profit Base, Tax Sheltering Activity, and the Changing Nature of Employee Compensation* by Mihir Desai, NBER Working Paper no. 8866 (2002).

7   *The Economic Implications of Corporate Financial Reporting* by John R. Graham, Campbell R. Harvey and Shiva Rajgopal (2004).

Chapter 7

TAX AVOIDANCE

SPEED-READ SUMMARY

■ Tax systems pose a constant ethical test to individuals and corporations.

■ Government demands for increased tax revenues to finance high public spending have led to growing resort to tax avoidance. The legislative response to this has caused tax systems to become more complex, which in turn makes ethical dilemmas more difficult.

■ A key ethical distinction is whether there is a genuine business purpose to a transaction that reduces the tax bill, or whether the transaction is entirely artificial. But the distinction is often far from clear cut.

■ Where directors have a legal obligation to maximise shareholder value they have an acute conflict of interest between the need to minimise the tax bill to satisfy shareholders and the need to do what is right and just with the tax authorities.

■ An aggressive approach to tax planning can entail reputational risk since both governments and the public expect companies to stump up for public expenditure.

■ For advisers, reputational risk is an even more serious issue. The experience of KPMG in the US, explored in this chapter, shows how one of the giants of the accountancy profession was severely damaged as a result of an over-aggressive approach to tax avoidance.

Tax systems constantly put the morality of individuals and the social responsibility of corporations to the test. They depend to a high degree on voluntary compliance and honesty in the provision by the taxpayer of information to governments. For their part governments have an obligation to ensure that there is clarity for taxpayers over what is regarded as fraudulent and what is acceptable in the cause of reducing their tax bill. Yet in practice very little is simple when it comes to the morality of taxation.

Back in 1929 the British judge Lord Clyde remarked: "No man in this country is under the smallest obligation, moral or other, so to arrange his legal relations to his business or his property as to enable the Inland Revenue to put the largest possible shovel into his stores." Underpinning that view is the belief that taxation is an interference in the citizen's right to enjoy property, which is justified in so far as it accords with the law.

Yet the inexorable rise in public spending in relation to gross domestic product across the developed world over the past century has caused tax bills to escalate to levels that have prompted questions about the legitimacy of taxation. In response to the growing pressure to meet governmental demands for increased revenue, more people have tried to keep the tax authorities' shovel out of their stores and more complexity has crept into the system as they resort to tax avoidance. This in turn means that the ethical dilemmas become more tricky, as tax law fails to keep up with the ingenious professional advisers and financiers who devise intricate trading strategies that increasingly make use of complex derivative instruments such as swaps, warrants and options for avoidance purposes.

There are broader moral issues at stake, too. The progressivity of the tax system, which reflects the democratic choice of the electorate, can be eroded as avoidance becomes more widespread. Against that, proponents of public choice theory argue that the more avoidance that takes place the better, because the rise in public spending reflects a political marketplace in which politicians bribe the electorate with expensive public policy proposals to win votes, while bureaucrats use public spending to build empires and maximise their personal utility. On this view, avoidance operates as a check and balance on rent seeking, the economists' jargon for extracting high value from a commodity that is in fixed supply. Yet in practice governments have responded to the greater ingenuity of tax avoidance practitioners by resorting to retrospective taxation.

Even the language of taxation has become confused and confusing. Under Lord Clyde's dictum it was possible to think in terms of a clear distinction between evasion, which was illegal, and avoidance, which was legal. Yet avoidance has acquired a pejorative connotation since New Zealand enacted legislation in 1995 that introduced a concept of "abusive" avoidance. Taking an abusive tax position in New Zealand means that the taxpayer embarks on an artificial avoidance strategy without having a reasonably arguable position that no tax is due. This terminology is now being used in many other jurisdictions, including the US and UK. So some people argue that it is helpful to refer to tax mitigation rather than avoidance when talking about legitimate means of reducing the tax burden.

A QUESTION OF PURPOSE

A central question, whether for managers or individuals, is the purpose of transactions that reduce the tax bill. Many would argue that if there is no genuine business purpose and that transactions are undertaken exclusively to reduce taxes, the strategy is unethical. In some jurisdictions, most notably the US, the courts have taken that view. Yet the ethical dilemma can be more tricky. For companies, tax is a cost that has a hugely important bearing on the bottom line of the profit and loss account. As well as an obligation to ensure the company pays taxes as required by law, managers, most notably in the English-speaking jurisdictions, have a legal obligation to maximise value for shareholders. They are thus subject to a pressing conflict of interest.

Some respond by taking a stand on the strict letter of the tax law and adopt a policy of aggressive tax mitigation. There is ample evidence that resort to the use of such artificial tax shelters has increased since the shareholder value movement swept the US and the Anglosphere economies in the 1990s. Others take the view that aggressive mitigation is anti-social because if everyone took that path, the tax base would be dangerously eroded. It is, after all, an inescapable fact that the tax authorities will always have difficulty keeping abreast of the latest highly artificial device for tax avoidance. And if public opinion takes a poor view of companies that are very aggressive in their dealings with the tax authorities there may be a reputational risk in pursuing such a course. There can also be a financial risk if the revenue authorities disallow an artificial avoidance scheme that has reduced previous tax charges by a material amount such that current year earnings are subject to a big hit in the form of a prior year charge. So even those who do not acknowledge that moral issues arise in relation to artificial tax avoidance might still have to apply cost-benefit analysis to their strategy in the interests of shareholder value. A key question is whether it can be right to adopt a strategy that would undermine public policy if many others took the same path. Does the underlying philosophy really boil down to devil take the hindmost?

THE PROFESSIONALS

The moral dilemmas are acute in the advisory fraternity, where accountants, lawyers and other professionals have to decide how far, if at all, they can afford to take a moral line in peddling aggressive tax mitigation strategies. In practice, they tend to pass the buck to the client. When pitching in competition for tax business before the audit committees of quoted companies, professionals often ask the potential clients where on the spectrum they wish to position themselves, running from tame acquiescence in the spirit of the law at one extreme, to intense aggression in the use of tax shelters at the other. But for some, the question may even be whether to invite the client to risk violating the law. Nowhere has this been better illustrated than at the US practice of KPMG, one of the Big Four auditing firms, which was heavily involved in mass marketing highly artificial tax products in the 1990s.

KPMG'S TAX SHELTERS

KPMG was slow to go into the mass marketing of tax shelters. It had a wake-up call when it entered into abortive merger talks with Ernst & Young, where negotiations revealed to KPMG's partners how much more lucrative Ernst & Young's tax practice was than their own. They very swiftly made it a priority to build their tax practice so that by 2002 revenues from tax services accounted for a much higher proportion of the firm's total revenue than at the other four of the Big Five firms. Because the US Senate Permanent Subcommittee on Investigations launched an investigation in 2003, it is possible to see how the firm's partners and employees dealt with the dilemmas through the internal emails that were thrown up by the investigation.

The following email, sent to Jeffrey Stein, then the head of KPMG's tax practice, by Gregg Ritchie, who ran a working group whose job was to develop tax shelters, makes an extraordinary case study. It concerns a product known as OPIS, which involved artificial share and loan transactions conducted offshore via a Cayman Island company, with the assistance of Deutsche Bank, lawyers Brown & Wood, a securities outfit called Quadra and a tax advisory boutique called Presidio. The purpose was to generate losses to offset gains made by KPMG's individual clients in the stock market bubble of the late 1990s, including gains made in Silicon Valley and elsewhere on the exercise of stock options. Each sale of OPIS was expected to generate a fee of $360,000 on average for the firm. Along with two other similar products known as FLIP and BLIPS, this earned KPMG fees of nearly $100m between 1996 and 2000, according to the Senate Subcommittee investigation.

The central question the email addresses is whether the firm should register the strategy in advance with the US Internal Revenue Service, as required by law.

KPMG Peat Marwick LLP

```
Date:      May 26, 1998
To:        Jeffrey N.Stein
From:      Gregg Ritchie
           Los Angeles/Woodland Hills
           Steno:gwr
RefP:      \\users\green\vp\cats\ppts\cl.doc
Cc:        Distribution List
```

▶

OPIS Tax Shelter Registration

Attached is a memorandum from Jeff Zysik (Tax Innovation Center) concerning the potential financial consequences associated with failing to register a tax shelter under IRC section 6111. For purposes of this discussion, I will assume that we conclude that the OPIS product meets the definition of a tax shelter under IRC section 6111(c).

Based on this assumption the following are my conclusions and recommendation as to why KPMG should make the business/strategic decision not to register the OPIS product as a tax shelter. My conclusions and resulting recommendation are based upon the immediate negative impact on the Firm's strategic initiative to develop a sustainable tax products practice and the long term implications of establishing a precedent in registering such a product.

First, the financial exposure to the Firm is minimal. Based upon our analysis of the applicable penalty sections, we conclude that the penalties would be no greater than $14,000 per $100,000 in KPMG fees. Furthermore, as the size of the deal increases, our exposure to the penalties decreases as a percentage of our fees. For example, our average deal would result in KPMG fees of $360,000 with a maximum penalty exposure of only $31,000.

This further assumes that KPMG would bear 100 per cent of the penalty. In fact, as explained in the attached memo, the penalty is joint and several with respect to anyone involved in the product who was required to register. Given that, at a minimum, Presidio would also be required to register, our share of the penalties could be viewed as being only one half of the amounts noted above. If other OPIS participants (e.g. Deutsche Bank, Brown & Wood, etc.) were also found to be promoters subject to the registration requirements, KPMG's exposure would be further minimized. Finally, any ultimate exposure to the penalties are abatable if it can be shown that we had reasonable cause.

Second, the rules under section 6111(c) have not changed significantly since they were imposed in 1984. While there was an addition to section 6111 in the 1997 Tax Act, it only applies to products marketed to corporate investors under limited circumstances. To my knowledge, the Firm has never registered a product under section 6111.

Third, the tax community at large continues to avoid registration of all products. Based on my knowledge, the representations made by Presidio and Quadra, and Larry DeLap's discussions with his counterparts of the Big 6 firms, there are no tax products marketed to individuals by our competitors which are registered. This includes income conversion strategies, loss generation techniques, and other related strategies.

Should KPMG decide to begin to register its tax products, I believe that it will position us with a severe competitive disadvantage in light of industry norms to such degree that we will not be able to compete in the tax advantaged products market.

Fourth, there has been (and, apparently, continues to be) a lack of enthusiasm on the part of the Service to enforce section 6111. In speaking with KPMG individuals who were at the Service (e.g.Richard Smith), the Service has apparently purposefully ignored enforcement efforts related to section 6111. In informal discussions with individuals currently at the Service, WNT has confirmed that there are not many registration applications submitted and they do not have the resources to dedicate to this area.

Finally, the guidance from Congress, the Treasury, and the Service is minimal, unclear, and extremely difficult to interpret when attempting to apply it to "tax planning" products. The Code section, regulations and related material were clearly written with a view toward the sale of a partnership interest by a promoter which purports to allow an investor to claim deductions significantly in excess of their investment. While the rules are written broadly enough to arguably include OPIS and other purely tax planning products, they are not easily applied to the marketing of an idea or strategy to a client which carries with it tax advantage.

Although OPIS includes the purchase of securities by the investor, the tax results are driven simply by an interpretation of the application of Code section 302 and the regulations thereunder. When coupled with the Service's apparent lack of

➤

enforcement effort, the lack of specific guidance is a further indication that the risk of non-compliance with the rules could be excused.

Based on the above arguments, it is my recommendation that KPMG does not register the OPIS product as a tax shelter. Any financial exposure that may be applicable can easily be dealt with by setting up a reserve against fees collected. Given the relatively nominal amount of such potential penalties, the Firm's financial results should not be affected by this decision.

In summary, I believe that the rewards of a successful marketing of the OPIS product (and the competitive disadvantages which may result from registration) far exceed the financial exposure to penalties that may arise. Once you have had an opportunity to review this information, I request that we have a conference with the persons on the distribution list (and any other relevant parties) to come to a conclusion with respect to my recommendations. As you know, we must immediately deal with this issue in order to proceed with the OPIS product.

Distribution List:
Mark Springer
Doug Ammerman
Walter Duer

Proprietary Material
Confidentiality Requested
KPMG[1]

A SHOCKING STRATEGY

One striking feature here is that the moral issue is straightforwardly black and white. The email proposes a potentially illegal course of action on the basis of a purely financial cost-benefit calculus: if KPMG is caught, the cost of the penalties will fall short of the fees already earned. Another striking feature is that morality does not come into it at any point. The writer draws comfort from the fact that KPMG has never registered a product under this section of the law before, which is a dubious justification for any course of action.

He says that everyone else is doing it, so failure to do it would result in competitive disadvantage. And he feels that the firm will probably get away with it; and since the law is unclear, there is a handy excuse if KPMG finds itself in the dock.

That one of the big professional accountancy firms could have sanctioned such a clearly unethical and potentially illegal business strategy undoubtedly shocked the Senate Subcommittee on Investigations. It testifies to the decline in the professional ethos that resulted from the progressive commercialisation of the accountancy profession and also reflects the more widespread drop in standards that accompanied the stock market bubble of the 1990s. Mass marketing is simply not compatible with the objectivity and independence that are supposed to be the hallmark of the professional firm. In fairness to KPMG it should be said that other big firms were doing the same thing. As the facts emerged, the senior partners recognised that there had been inadequate supervision. Jeffrey Stein, who had moved up to be deputy chairman of the firm, was removed along with all those responsible. Since the episode KPMG has cleaned up its risk-management procedures and tried to raise its ethical standards.

That said, the episode points to an important question that crops up very frequently in business. If everyone else is doing something unethical, it is often said that the firm will forfeit competitive advantage if it fails to go along. Yet this can be a very short-term definition of competitive disadvantage which completely overlooks reputational risks. This particular story firmly underlines the point. The big accountancy firms were subsequently forced into expensive settlements with the IRS, accompanied by much bad publicity, over their tax shelters. KPMG found itself in deeper trouble because it initially refused to hand over documents to the authorities on grounds of client confidentiality. When it lost its court case on the issue it was obliged to cooperate. Clients sued it, alleging fraud and negligent misrepresentation. And the Department of Justice started an investigation, giving rise to speculation that KPMG might disintegrate as Andersen had done after the Enron debacle.

The implicit threat from the DoJ was arguably disproportionate, since

KPMG's tax practice for individuals was not a core part of the firm's business. For the senior partners the sums involved in the sales of these tax shelters were peanuts. That underlines the vital importance of understanding reputational risk. At KPMG the reputational damage from all this was formidable because it found itself at the centre of the largest criminal tax case ever filed. The firm eventually admitted to criminal wrongdoing and had to agree to pay $456 million in fines, restitution and penalties as part of a deal to defer prosecution. In addition, six former KPMG partners and the former deputy chairman, Jeffrey Stein, were criminally prosecuted for what the Department of Justice called a multi-billion-dollar criminal tax fraud conspiracy involving the generation of at least $11 billion of phoney tax losses at a cost to the US government of at least $2.5 billion in evaded taxes. KPMG also admitted that its personnel deliberately concealed the existence of shelters from the IRS, not only by failing to register the shelters as required by law, but by fraudulently concealing the shelter losses and income on tax returns and attempting to hide the shelters using sham attorney–client privilege claims. The firm also suffered the ignominy of having to install an independent government-appointed monitor to oversee its compliance with the deferred prosecution agreement for three years, as well as being subject to permanent restrictions on its tax practice.

From a public-interest perspective, the consequences of KPMG's behaviour were potentially very damaging. If the DoJ had pursued the firm as vigorously as it had pursued Andersen, the Big Four audit firms would have come down to three, leading to much reduced competition in the market for auditing. The damaging press headlines may also have contributed to a wider loss of confidence in the accountancy profession and heightened the concern among lawmakers and in the Public Company Accounting Oversight Board over the conflicts of interest inherent in auditors passing judgement on the tax liabilities of companies that had bought their own highly artificial and abusive avoidance schemes. The irony is that if KPMG, or any of the others, had been prepared to forgo some short-term loss of competitive advantage, their competitive position would have been greatly enhanced when everyone else's chickens came home to roost.

On the fundamental issue, with or without the benefit of hindsight, there is no room for doubt. Any firm that allows its people to embark on a potentially illegal course on the Machiavellian justification that they will come out on top financially, even if caught, must be considered ethically deficient or incompetent, or both. It has to be said that there are industries – waste management is one that springs to mind – where many managers regard criminal investigations into the business as a normal operating cost. But the professions are different, not least because they enjoy exemptions and privileges. The big accountancy firms, for example, usually have the benefit of a captive clientele thanks to the statutory requirement on all but the smallest companies to undergo an annual audit. The public is thus entitled to expect high ethical standards of professional firms, as are the firms' clients. Yet the opportunistic sale of aggressive tax shelters by KPMG and others in the late 1990s demonstrates that professionals are as prone to ethical lapses as the rest of the business community when markets become overheated. Nothing could better illustrate how integrity waxes and wanes according to the vicissitudes of the economic cycle.

➤ QUESTIONS FOR DIRECTORS AND FINANCE EXECUTIVES

1. Does the board have a policy setting out the company's approach to tax planning? Is it made publicly available?

2. Does the policy have an ethical content, or does it boil down to expediency/devil take the hindmost?

3. If you have an obligation to maximise shareholder value, does this mean there is no alternative but to engage in extremely artificial transactions for the exclusive purpose of tax mitigation? Or is it legitimate simply to do whatever transactions the company needs to do to further its business in a tax-efficient manner?

4. If everyone else adopted the same approach to tax planning as you, would it result in public policy being undermined?

➤

5. Is there a reputational risk in the tax policy you have adopted?

6. Do you report on the tax charge and your approach to tax planning in the annual report in a way that gives shareholders some indication of the degree of risk in the company's policy?

➤ QUESTIONS FOR ADVISERS

1. Do you regard the degree of aggression in tax planning as an ethical issue for the client rather than the adviser? If you do, is this an abdication of moral responsibility? Are you sure you are not failing to honour your duty of care to the client in taking such a view? And are you underestimating the reputational risk to your firm inherent in this position?

2. Do you have an explicit policy on your approach to tax planning? Have you made sure that your fellow partners in the non-tax areas of the firm understand it and grasp the inherent risks? Is the policy publicly available?

3. Have you made clear to your clients the nature and extent of the risks they are running with tax avoidance schemes? Are you sure they understand them? Would you recommend the schemes to your own close family or use them yourself?

4. If you operate in a system where pre-notification of tax avoidance schemes applies, are you sure your judgement is not biased against notifying?

5. In selling tax avoidance schemes, are you sure you are not putting your own financial interests and those of the firm before those of the clients?

NOTES

1   From the Report titled "U.S. Tax Shelter Industry: The Role of Accountants, Lawyers, And Financial Professionals", prepared by the Minority Staff of the Permanent Subcommittee on Investigations, released in conjunction with the Permanent Subcommittee on Investigation's hearings on 18 and 20 November 2003. For full transcript, <www.senate.gov/~govt-aff/_files/sprt10834tax_shelters.pdf>.

Chapter 8

WHISTLEBLOWING

SPEED-READ SUMMARY

- More than any other issue in business ethics, whistleblowing raises the question of whether ethical standards can be applied on a global basis.

- Whistleblowers in any culture face an acute conflict of interest between the duties of confidentiality and loyalty to the company and the need to uphold the public interest or the interests of stakeholders such as consumers, employees and the tax authorities.

- In consensual cultures such as Japan whistleblowing is seen by many as an unthinkable breach of mutual obligations within the community of the corporation.

- In the more individualistic US whistleblowing is more often regarded as an essential safety valve and form of internal control which has the potential to pre-empt financial damage of the kind that overtook Enron and other corporate casualties, although many business leaders continue to view whistleblowers as malcontents.

- Across the world there is a spectrum of attitudes, but the trend is towards convergence on the more positive view of whistleblowing.

- The dilemma for employees is to strike the right balance between the conflicting duties of loyalty to the company and public interest, as well as between the duty to the employee's family versus possible career suicide.

- The biggest problem with whistleblowing is that the companies in which it would be of most value are likely to be ones where the corporate culture is both fundamentally flawed and hostile to the practice.

Nothing more clearly demonstrates the cultural differences in business ethics across the world than attitudes to whistleblowing. Merely to define the practice is to underline the intractability of the ethical dilemmas involved. In the definition of British author Gerald Vinten, whistleblowing is "the unauthorised disclosure of information that an employee reasonably believes evidences the contravention of any law, rule or regulation, code of practice, or professional statement, or that involves mismanagement, corruption, abuse of authority, or danger to public or worker health and safety".[1] So we run into tricky questions as to when it is appropriate for an employee to flout authority and disclose. What is reasonable belief, especially when most potential whistleblowers usually have access only to partial information about the wrongdoing? What constitutes mismanagement and how well placed is the employee to make judgements about it? How great is the danger to the public or to employees relative to the damage that may be done to the company's reputation and workplace relations? And when is it justifiable to go beyond internal whistleblowing and disclose information to regulators, police or the media? The one thing in this area that is beyond dispute is that potential whistleblowers in any culture face an acute conflict of interest between the duties of confidentiality and loyalty to the firm and the need to uphold the public interest or the interests of stakeholders such as consumers, employees and shareholders. But attitudes about where to strike the balance in dealing with that conflict vary enormously.

At one extreme is Japan, a society which values consensual behaviour in the workplace and where people have an extreme aversion to open conflict. These characteristics are deeply rooted. The 6th-century constitution prepared by Japan's first lawgiver, Taishi Shotoku, emphasised the Japanese concept of harmony, which has a much broader range of meanings than the English word, and urged the people to "regard harmony as noble, and non-contrariness as honourable".[2] Japanese society is also imbued with the Confucian respect for authority and hierarchy. From their schooldays onwards the Japanese are encouraged not to stand out. Note, too, that in Japanese schools the pupil who is bullied is often deemed to be the one at fault – a point very relevant in the present context since most whistleblowers suffer heavy penalties at the hands of their employers for their unauthorised actions and may be ostracised by fellow employees.

For the Japanese, a large company is a community run in the interests of employees rather than shareholders. So non-consensual behaviour such as whistleblowing is perceived as a near-unthinkable breach of mutual obligations tantamount to betrayal. Nor is there much understanding of how blowing the whistle might actually help the company. In post-war Japan, industrial success has been greatly enhanced by the practice of kaizen, or continuous improvement, whereby employees constantly make suggestions about how productivity can be enhanced. Management rightly sees the workforce as a valuable source of information and ideas. The consensual approach to corporate strategy and implementation also operates as a kind of substitute for the checks and balances on which large Western companies more heavily rely. Yet the process of kaizen accommodates only positive suggestions. It does not encourage negative comments on things that are going wrong in the company. And for as long as lifetime employment was an entrenched feature of the big company ethos in Japan, a whistleblowing employee had more at stake than a whistleblower in the much more flexible labour market conditions in the US.

The attitude to consumer protection and public safety in Japan appears at odds with Western views. In the post-war period the powerful bureaucrats and businessmen who ran Japan Inc. established a distinctive model of export-led growth. Export success was perceived to be a far more important priority than providing satisfaction to Japanese consumers. If public health suffered as a result of industrial activity, the bureaucrats were often disinclined to be punitive to the company responsible. There have been notorious cases where, for example, the Ministry of Health, Labour and Welfare, which heavily protects the Japanese pharmaceutical industry, has colluded with companies in covering up the deaths of people killed by the side effects of new drugs. There have also been cases where whistleblowers, on the rare occasions when they do emerge, have disclosed wrongdoing to industry regulators whose immediate reaction was to inform the whistleblowers' employers.

THE COST OF KEEPING QUIET

Against that background, it is not entirely surprising that there have been high-profile examples of public safety and consumer protection scandals where no one blew the whistle. Among the more notorious was the nuclear leak at Tokaimura in a plant operated by a subsidiary of Sumitomo Metal Mining Company. In processing highly enriched uranium for an experimental fast-breeder reactor the workers had been using procedures that had been illegally modified. Instead of using high-tech equipment, they dumped the uranium manually into steel buckets. It reached critical mass and exploded into uncontrolled nuclear fission, causing the world's worst nuclear accident since Chernobyl. Management had failed to give the workers any understanding of the risks involved. The regulators were subsequently shown to have been grossly incompetent and no local hospitals were equipped to handle victims exposed to radiation. Despite many people being aware that illegal procedures were being followed, nobody blew the whistle.

So, too, with the cover-up that took place at Mitsubishi Motors. In 2000 the police discovered that the company was keeping a covert set of records in which customer complaints were hidden from the regulatory authorities. The regulators were fed with wholly false information for no less than 23 years. When the existence of this dual set of books was uncovered, 700,000 cars had to be recalled for defects, including faulty brakes and fuel leaks. In the same year a similar horror story emerged at the dairy company Snow Brand, which managed to poison 14,000 people with tainted milk as a result of faulty health and safety procedures that had been defective for years. The failure to blow the whistle in such cases is a clear reflection of the presiding business culture. When a survey conducted by Hisatake Kato, a professor of ethics at Kyoto University, asked workers in Tokyo if they would disclose wrongdoing in their company, 99 per cent said they would not.[3]

At the other extreme is the US, where whistleblowers have been turned into Hollywood heroes and can find themselves glamorised on the cover of *Time* magazine. Whistleblowing sits easily with the free speech tradition of the First Amendment and the individualistic American culture. In fact, the practice of blowing the whistle has been sanctioned in law since the False Claims Act, passed in 1863 during the Civil War to cope with widespread military procurement fraud. The legislation gave private citizens the right to bring an action on their own behalf as well as on behalf of the US government and also provides an incentive to do so. Today, in the revised version of this Act, the whistleblower can receive up to 25 per cent of the judgement if the government joins the suit and the case is successful. Nor is this the only rewards-based whistleblowing scheme. The Financial Institutions Reform, Recovery and Enforcement Act, which made provisions for the bailout of the savings and loans in the 1980s, included incentives for people to disclose.

For Americans, unlike the Japanese, the corporation is seen more as a legal construct than a community. And the ease with which companies can fire employees in the US means that, by contrast with many continental European countries or Japan, whistleblowers need greater legal protection. Since the National Labor Relations Act of 1935, the first such legislation, anti-reprisal laws have proliferated in areas such as the environment, health and safety, civil rights and labour relations and include the Whistleblower Protection Act of 1978. Private watchdog organisations such as the Government Accountability Project provide support, notably via the internet, for whistleblowers. At one level, blowing the whistle is increasingly seen as a patriotic and social duty which promotes accountability through the public's right to know. At another, inside firms, the practice is seen as an early warning resource and a supplement to conventional internal control. There is also a trend towards imposing a duty to whistleblow in certain circumstances. A recent case in point is the Sarbanes-Oxley Act, which in the aftermath of the raft of corporate scandals in the US, imposed a legal duty on the company's lawyers to disclose wrongdoing and sought to encourage anonymous whistleblowing in relation to misconduct that threatened shareholder value.

SUCCESSES AND FAILURES

Viewed in this light, the value of whistleblowing is particularly great in the financial area, where high leverage and the risk of deposit withdrawals make financial institutions more vulnerable to collapse than most non-financial companies. The constructive aspect emerged most clearly at National Australia Bank, where rogue traders' losses of A$180 million might have escalated much further without the intervention of a whistleblower. Australia also furnishes a classic example of the negative consequences of failing to heed a whistleblower. In 1999 and again in 2000 Jeffrey Simpson, a financial services manager at HIH Insurance, raised concerns that the company had breached minimum solvency requirements. He took his worries to the Institute of Chartered Accountants and to the Australian Prudential Regulation Authority, the pensions watchdog. Both bodies ignored him. HIH went into liquidation in 2001. While his action might not have prevented HIH's collapse if it had been heeded, it is likely that the losses incurred and the damage inflicted on policyholders would have been less if earlier action had been taken in response to his concerns.

It would be wrong to imply that whistleblowing is now non-controversial even in countries like the US. Many employers still see the whistleblower as an industrial malcontent rather than a good-faith backstop for the internal control system. Many employees fail to rise to what can be a very difficult and thankless challenge. At WorldCom, for example, the formal report of the Special Investigative Committee of the Board of Directors concluded: "That the fraud continued as long as it did was due to a lack of courage to blow the whistle on the part of others in WorldCom's financial and accounting department." Legal protections have failed to ensure that all employees who disclose in the public interest are spared reprisals. Even celebrity whistleblowers like Sherron Watkins, who alerted Enron's chairman Kenneth Lay to wrongdoing in the finance department, though in the event to no effect, cannot look forward to a conventional career after the publicity surrounding such action. And however positive a view management takes of the activity, the underlying conflict of interest is present in the US system just as it is in Japan. Moreover, the American courts will, in some circumstances, look at the trade-off between harmony and productivity in the workplace and the public interest and come down against the public-spirited employee. In *Smith* v. *Calgon*

Carbon Corporation in 1990 the US Court of Appeals for the Third Circuit held that the Pennsylvania Supreme Court would not entertain a wrong dismissal action by an employee who blew the whistle on an employer who polluted the air and water. The court held that "the public's countervailing interest in workplace harmony and productivity was more compelling, at least where the employee involved was not charged with the specific responsibilities of protecting the public's interest".

So to suggest that there is a clear polarisation between the US, where disclosure is seen as positive and silence as complicity, and Japan, where public-interest disclosure constitutes betrayal of the company, goes too far, especially since Japan has now embraced the notion of public-interest disclosure legislation. Nor, if we look at the developed world, is there a well-defined spectrum between these two poles on which individual countries can be neatly fitted. In Asia, for example, the current predominant business model is the family company. Whistleblowing has less relevance in this context than in larger, more impersonal corporate bureaucracies where ownership is divorced from control. Much the same is true in parts of continental Europe, where it is worth noting in passing that some institutions, such as the European Commission, have an in-built hostility to whistleblowing, despite a record of frequent budgetary waste and fraud. And in countries with a tradition of adversarial labour relations, such as Australia, the employee mindset may be less attuned to the notion of blowing the whistle in the company's interest. There is also a strong cultural antipathy for "dobbing", the Australian term for sneaking on others, which poses an obstacle to disclosing wrongdoing by fellow employees. In other countries such as France there is an equal and opposite tradition of sneaking on colleagues and neighbours by sending anonymous letters to the regulatory, police and tax authorities. Many of the corruption scandals that have surrounded French politicians over the past half century came to light as a result of this anonymous disclosure.

A GLOBAL TREND IN A WHISTLEBLOWING DIRECTION

Yet despite all the differences in attitude to whistleblowing, there does appear to be a global trend towards entrenching the practice in corporate life. The idea that it provides "an essential safety valve within the internal control environment", in the phrase used by the Institute of Chartered Accountants in England and Wales, is gaining ground.[4] And increasingly it is sanctioned in corporate governance codes. A typical case in point is the UK Combined Code which sets out the principles of corporate governance to be followed by British quoted companies. It states:

The audit committee should review arrangements by which staff of the company may, in confidence, raise concerns about possible improprieties in matters of financial reporting or other matters. The audit committee's objective should be to ensure that arrangements are in place for the proportionate and independent investigation of such matters and for appropriate follow-up action.

This is supported by the UK's Public Concern Disclosure Act. According to Guy Dehn, until recently Director of Public Interest at Work, a charity which had considerable input into the legislation, the Act was designed to signal a change in culture whereby organisations and society would be more likely to address the message rather than shoot the messenger.[5] It offers tiered protection for the whistleblower, depending on whether disclosure is internal, to a regulator, to the media and so forth, with the highest legal protections being offered for internal disclosure.

For some, including the Japanese, the biggest challenge will be to implement a law that runs profoundly counter to the current business culture and broader cultural categorical imperatives. It is worth pointing out in passing that the Japanese commercial code which lays down the legal basis for corporate life in Japan requires directors to look after the interests of shareholders. Yet in its operations the Japanese post-war economic model has worked on a very different presumption: companies have been run in the interests of directors and employees, with little thought being spared for the interests of outside shareholders. That said, many features of the model have broken down since the bursting of the Japanese bubble in the early 1990s. The accountability of management to a lead bank has eroded and new forms of checks and balances are needed. The various public safety and consumer non-protection scandals have also caused business and the bureaucracy to suffer a marked loss of legitimacy in the public perception. If Japanese business is not to find itself at the wrong end of an increasingly hostile public backlash, it has an interest of its own in the kind of safety valve offered by permitting employees to blow the whistle in the knowledge that they will not be penalised if they have acted in good faith.

For other countries the challenge for corporate managers and employees will include the problem of how to go beyond the letter of the law and instil a culture where responsible whistleblowing can play its part in pre-empting financial damage and mitigating reputational risk. That is primarily a leadership task, involving boards of directors and top managers in promoting the benefits of the practice throughout the organisation and reassuring employees that they will not be punished for justifiable whistleblowing. And it should not be forgotten that companies themselves have a role as whistleblowers in relation to corruption. Once again, good leadership is required to blow the whistle on government ministers or officials who could be a lucrative source of business to a company's less scrupulous competitors. Whether we are looking at the corporate governance scandals in the US or the public safety and consumer non-protection scandals in Japan, the case for responsible whistleblowing regardless of culture has surely been made. The dilemma for the employee, in terms of balancing the duties of loyalty and public interest, and duty to family versus possible career suicide, will always be acute. But for directors of companies, whistleblowing is an important and potentially useful resource that needs to be managed well. The overwhelming problem with the positive view is that in a company where whistleblowing is needed, things will usually have reached a pass where the culture is fundamentally flawed and management is most unlikely to take a positive view of the practice.

➤ CONCLUDING CHECKLIST FOR EMPLOYERS

1. Does the company have a stated policy on whistleblowing, compliant with the law, establishing channels of communication for individuals to report possible breaches of law, regulations, ethics codes, or mismanagement damaging to the company? Do channels of communication operate outside the line-management structure, so that employees can have confidence in the independence of the procedures for investigating their disclosures? Are the procedures reviewed by the audit committee?

2. Has top management fostered a culture in which employees know that they can safely raise concerns in good faith about wrongdoing, without risking victimisation or career damage? Does the culture ensure that loyalty is owed to the company, not the line manager?

3. Has the company indicated a proper way to raise concerns outside the company with helpline providers or other sources of independent advice?

4. Are training and management systems in place to support the whistleblowing policy?

5. If you, the top manager, were an employee lower down the organisation, would you have confidence in the company's whistleblowing procedures and regard them as a convincing alternative to resort to the media or other external avenues for disclosure of wrongdoing?

6. Are there appropriate penalties for making false or malicious allegations?

➤ CONCLUDING CHECKLIST FOR EMPLOYEES

1. How confident are you that you know sufficient facts to justify making a disclosure of wrongdoing that is potentially damaging to the company?

2. How competent are you to make a judgement about the extent of the damage to the company, or to stakeholders such as customers and the community, of the wrongdoing you are thinking of disclosing?

3. Have you properly weighed the potential damage to your relations with colleagues, your career and the potential financial and emotional strains on your family? Have you consulted appropriately in the family about the potential costs to other family members of whistleblowing?

4. Are you sure you are acting in good faith, and with reasonable grounds, to reveal a genuine threat to the company and to stakeholders, rather than pursuing a grievance or obsession?

5. If you are making an anonymous disclosure, are you sure it is because of a reasonable concern about victimisation rather than lack of confidence in the absolute validity of the disclosure about wrongdoing?

6. Have you researched the protections and penalties that will apply to you as a whistleblower under the law of the land?

7. Are you confident that the damage that could be done to the company as a result of external disclosure would be outweighed by the benefit to stakeholders and the public interest?

NOTES

1　Whistleblowing: Corporate Help or Hindrance? (*Management Decision*, 1992)

2　See *The Enigma of Japanese Power* by Karel van Wolferen (Vintage Books 1990), for a perceptive account of this aspect of Japanese culture.

3　Quoted in *Dogs And Demons – The Fall of Modern Japan*, by Alex Kerr (Penguin Books, 2001), which offers a stimulating interpretation of these scandals.

4　The phrase is from the ICAEW's guidance publications for audit committees.

5　See *Whistleblowing around the World – Law, Culture and Practice*, (Open Democracy Advice Centre and Public Concern at Work, 2004) eds. Richard Calland and Guy Dehn, for an informative discussion of many of the issues in this chapter.

Chapter 9

INDEPENDENT DIRECTORS

SPEED-READ SUMMARY

- As well as supporting the executives in driving the business forward, independent non-executives have an important monitoring role. They are required to protect shareholders where their interests conflict with those of self-interested or unethical managers.

- Independence requires that non-executives should be free from business or other relationships that would interfere with their judgement. Adherence to the definitions of independence contained in corporate governance codes or stock exchange listing rules often fails to prevent boards becoming clubby or being overtaken by corporate governance failure.

- Good governance ultimately depends on the competence and ethical integrity of individuals who serve on boards. These qualities are likely to become a more important focus of corporate governance in future, with greater emphasis being placed on whether nominees for the board have a "moral compass" that will help them do what is right for the company, its shareholders and the broader community.

Non-executive or outside directors have been a feature of company boards pretty much since the birth of the corporation. Yet the notion of the independent non-executive director only became an important focus of attention as a result of the divorce in the corporate world between ownership and control. This was identified in the 1930s by Berle and Means, who observed that companies were increasingly being run by professional managers on behalf of dispersed shareholders whose voting power was too fragmented for them to be able to hold the managers to account.[1] An agency problem is the result. As the 18th-century Scottish economist Adam Smith pointed out in *The Theory of Moral Sentiments*, markets cannot work well unless they operate within a moral framework. Yet he recognised in his much better-known work *The Wealth of Nations* that human nature will tend to ensure that an agent (manager) will never run the business as well as if he were the principal (shareholder). While the economist's view of agency theory can be criticised for understating the complexity of human motivation, there is undoubtedly widespread scope for the abuse of conflicts of interest between the self-interested manager and outside shareholders. To put it at its simplest, there is at the heart of the current incarnation of Anglo-American capitalism, a constant vulnerability to ethical lapses.

Governance practices, whether voluntary or imposed by regulation or law, have addressed this problem by making the board of directors the central mechanism for protecting investors against potential ethical failures of self-interested managers, as well as for monitoring management more generally and directing the company. In the Anglo-American world the law of fiduciary duty sets out what directors have to do to meet their responsibilities to the company and to investors. It imposes requirements for directors to act in good faith and with due care, loyalty and candour. Provided directors act within these concepts they enjoy protection through such legal devices as the US business judgement rule from having decisions second-guessed or overturned by the courts. At the same time governance codes and private sector best practice have entrenched the idea of the independent non-executive director. The overall goal is to protect investors while attracting their capital to the corporation.

Even in continental Europe, where the business model often incorporates a controlling shareholder rather than dispersed ownership, governance codes have recently placed increasing emphasis on the role of independent non-executives in protecting minority investors. So, too, in Asia. While the family firm remains the dominant business model there, listed companies in most of the larger Asian economies are now required to have independent non-executives. The impetus came from the Asian financial crisis of 1997, which prompted governance reforms across the region. Only in Japan are independent non-executives still a rarity. According to GovernanceMetrics International, which compiles data on governance practices across the world, some 70 per cent of Japanese boards consist entirely of insiders, while a mere 5 per cent of directors at the top 400 companies are independent.[2] This reflects the firm belief of many leading Japanese businessmen that the emphasis on shareholder value is an undesirable US import that threatens the Japanese view of the corporation as a community run primarily in the interests of the directors and employees.

Yet even the Japanese seem likely to move further in the direction of US practice on this score thanks to the erosion of the old Japanese governance system in which a main bank, working within a loose-knit keiretsu group of companies, played an important role in holding companies to account and replacing management when performance faltered. Since the Japanese banking crisis of the 1990s, banks have been reducing their equity stakes in client companies. Business links and cross-shareholdings between keiretsu companies have weakened. Much of the traditional governance approach has thus been destroyed, leaving a vacuum that will have to be filled by some other means. Already there are signs that boards of leading Japanese companies are becoming less ceremonial in character. At the time of writing the country's Financial Services Agency is expected to introduce requirements for independent outside directors.

DEFINITION OF INDEPENDENCE

What is the definition of independence in the context of the boardroom? The UK Cadbury Committee on corporate governance in the early 1990s defined independence for non-executive directors as being "free from any business or other relationship which could materially interfere with the exercise of their independent judgement". This is a good practical definition. But relationships can be hard to pin down and interference with the exercise of independent judgement may be a subtle process not easily identified. Most CEOs like to have other CEOs on their boards because they are more likely to see the CEO's point of view on any given issue. In countries where the non-executives have a dual role, acting in effect as both player and referee, non-executives tend to have a strong desire to be supportive of the CEO. Human instinct dictates that the support role comes more naturally to people than the checking, balancing and evaluating roles. So even if there is no ostensible business or other relationship between such non-executives and the CEO and nothing that constitutes an explicit ethical lapse, the boardroom may nonetheless be a clubby place that operates as a poor check on the executive management of the company.

Interesting data on this comes from a recent academic study in the US. It shows how back-door links falling short of relationships conventionally regarded as undermining independence may play an important role in influencing CEO compensation. According to the researchers' calculations in a sample of 3,114 firms and 22,074 directors, CEOs who had any back-door link via boardroom connections to someone on the compensation committee received on average $453,688 more than CEOs with no such links. The average compensation for CEOs at firms where inside and outside directors were linked in any way was greater by $612,422.[3] There could, of course, be innocent explanations for this, such as non-executive directors having access to better information about compensation methodologies and comparisons thanks to their corporate social networks. All the same, the figures are suggestive.

CLUBBINESS

The response in many countries to the problem of clubbiness in the boardroom has been to formalise the appointment of non-executive directors by putting the task in the hands of a nomination committee consisting mainly or exclusively of independent non-executives. Increasing emphasis is now placed on independent board leadership, either by splitting the roles of chairman and chief executive, or appointing a senior independent director. In the US there has also been a determined attempt to incorporate in stock exchange listing agreements very detailed definitions of what business relationships cannot be construed as independent, together with definitions of materiality in transactions between the company and its directors. In many countries the law or governance codes put a limit on how long a non-executive can be regarded as independent. And in Italy and Sweden outside institutional shareholders have been brought into the decision-making process on board appointments.

AMERICAN INTERNATIONAL GROUP

Yet even with these safeguards in place it is striking how often corporate governance failure is accompanied by telltale signs that the non-executive directors' independence may be in question even if the rules have been complied with. A case in point is American International Group, where Maurice "Hank" Greenberg was for many years the prototypical overdominant chairman and chief executive until the New York State Attorney General, Eliot Spitzer, attacked the group with allegations that it had dishonestly manipulated its financial statements. The board of AIG was undeniably clubby. Half the outside directors were members or directors with Mr Greenberg of the Council on Foreign Relations, an independent policy forum. The Starr Foundation, a non-profit organisation controlled by Mr Greenberg, gave money to bodies with which AIG non-executives were involved. A big recipient of Starr funds was the Asia Society where AIG non-executive Richard Holbrooke, former US ambassador to the United Nations, was a trustee alongside Mr Greenberg, as well as chairman of the society's executive committee. The American Museum of Natural History, where AIG non-executive Ellen Futter was president, received more than $26m. The Institute for International Economics, with which another non-executive, Carla Hills, the former US trade representative, was associated, received $3.2m. And there were many more of this kind.[4]

There is no suggestion of impropriety here. Under the rules AIG was able to say that its directors could be considered independent if contributions to not-for-profit corporations they ran did not exceed $1m or 2 per cent of the charitable organisation's gross revenues for the most recent year. And the non-executive directors could argue that when information emerged about the misleading accounts after Eliot Spitzer's investigations they fired Mr Greenberg. Yet that still leaves the question of whether the non-executives were sufficiently independent to provide a proper check and balance before the attorney general intervened. Similar points could be made about Enron, where some non-executive directors had consultancy contracts with the company, and countless others where corporate governance failures took place.

INGREDIENTS OF GOOD CORPORATE GOVERNANCE

Perhaps the biggest difficulty over independence in the boardroom is that it is never a sufficient condition to ensure good corporate governance and performance. First, because non-executive directors suffer from an information disadvantage vis-à-vis the executives. They cannot perform well if the executives feed them only carefully filtered information. Even if the non-executives do have enough information that does not mean that their input will be put to good use. Prue Leith, a serial non-executive director in the UK, has disarmingly admitted: "In 20 years, on a good fistful of top plc (public limited company) boards, I suspect I have served no purpose whatever. Or rather, I have served no purpose that I could not have served as a consultant – better served, since CEOs tend to listen to consultants and ignore their non-executive directors."[5] No doubt others would claim to have been more successful. Yet the job calls for an exceptional degree of experience and judgement. It is important that it should be done by independent-minded people for whom forfeiting the directors' fees would never be a matter of concern if resignation was the right course of action. To be effective, non-executives need the insight and sufficient access to gain a sense of what motivates people in the company, what behaviour is rewarded and what the culture is all about.

IMPORTANCE OF CULTURE

Business culture is also important in a broader sense. In France, for example, non-executive directors have traditionally not performed the role of challenging the all-powerful président directeur général because this was simply not done. If substantial disagreement arose the non-executive would resign. Moreover, circumstances can easily conspire to make non-executives feel a strong obligation to support a wayward CEO. Vivendi Universal, which provided a platform for Jean-Marie Messier to embark on a notorious and near-ruinous acquisition spree, offers an intriguing case in point. Messier sat on the boards of many of the companies run by Vivendi's non-executives. The non-executives' independence was further eroded by incestuous business relationships between Vivendi and their companies. Yet these mattered less as Vivendi came close to bankruptcy than a sense of national solidarity when a minority of North American non-executives led by Edgar Bronfman Jr tried to oust Messier from the board. Whatever their doubts about their megalomaniac CEO, he was a French megalomaniac and they gave him nationalistic support even though he was a threat to the company's survival. It is difficult, or impossible, to draft governance codes to deal with such factors.

That underlines the fundamental point that good governance is ultimately dependent on the quality and ethical integrity of the individuals who people boards. Ira Millstein, the American lawyer and governance pioneer who drafted the first governance guidelines for the board of General Motors, puts it like this:

Fiduciary duties, new structures and processes, tone at the top, information flow and independent leadership do not fully assure us of the trust we need that directors will "do the right thing" when faced with the inevitable tough issues, such as compensation. Corporate governance must, and will, move beyond focusing on structural requirements to the more amorphous concepts such as honesty, loyalty, integrity and ethics. This will occur because the passage of time has shown that laundry lists of "must dos" can never spell out how a director should respond to every situation presented. Corporate governance best practice should and will require directors to be hard-wired to "do the right thing" in every aspect of decision making... Individual rights, such as corporations and their boards and managers enjoy in the market, require significant personal individual responsibilities. Board structures and processes are necessary but not sufficient... box ticking will not substitute for character.
The challenge going forward will be how to identify whether each person

being nominated and elected as a director possesses the character and individual "moral compass" which will allow him or her to do what is best for the company, investors and the broader community. Armed with this fresh "moral compass" perspective, the private sector and corporate governance scholars now need to think hard about how such directors can be identified objectively. Once this occurs, the pendulum can safely begin a swing back to Adam Smith's ethical man as the primary safeguard of efficient markets, a situation which is infinitely more preferable than markets capsizing under the weight of more and more government regulation. Directors with demonstrable moral compasses have little to fear in the courtroom, as the courts are inclined to seek out and identify ethical qualities and are less likely to impose liability upon a person who is thought to possess them.

That statement from one of the world's most influential governance experts puts corporate governance in its true ethical context.

➤ QUESTIONS FOR DIRECTORS ON ETHICS AND GOVERNANCE

1. Have you taken into account qualities such as ethical integrity in considering nominations to the board and the balance of the board?

2. Have you considered whether the non-executives are genuinely independent, as opposed to being compliant with governance codes and stock exchange listing requirements?

3. Are you striking the right balance between the dual roles of supporting the executives in driving the business forward and monitoring the executives to ensure that conflicts of interest with the shareholders are properly handled?

4. If there is a dominant shareholder, have you recognised that any move that disadvantages minority shareholders could be unethical and have you raised it on the board?

➤ QUESTIONS FOR DIRECTORS ON BOARD COMPENSATION

1. Are the rewards proposed for the executives overgenerous in relation to performance? Do they go beyond what is necessary to attract, retain and motivate individual executives?

2. Are boardroom pay consultants being used to put an imprimatur on excessive compensation, or are they making a genuine attempt to reach a solution that approximates to a market-type reward for the executive concerned?

3. Have you been sensitive to the impact of big boardroom pay awards on the workforce, especially where corporate performance has been poor or people are being laid off?

4. Where employees are granted stock options, have you considered whether they are appropriate and ensured that employees understand the risks in taking pay in this form?

5. If undisclosed elements of executives' pay packages were to be revealed in the media, would you find it hard to justify them?

● Case study:
DIRECTORS' PAY

If many people in North America and Europe feel the phrase "business ethics" comes close to being an oxymoron, it is chiefly because of spiralling boardroom pay. As so often, executives in the US have been at the forefront in exploring the limits of the law and, in recent years, the territory beyond. William McDonough, when president and CEO of the Federal Reserve Bank of New York, pointed to the ethical dimension of the problem in a speech at Trinity Church in Lower Manhattan on the first anniversary of the terrorist attacks on the Twin Towers.

I believe there is one issue in particular which requires corrective action. A recent study shows that, 20 years ago, the average chief executive officer of a publicly traded company made 42 times more than the average production worker. Perhaps one could justify that by the additional education required, the greater dedication, perhaps even the harder work. The same study shows that the average present day CEO makes over 400 times the average employee's income.

It is hard to find somebody more convinced than I of the superiority of the American economic system, but I can find nothing in economic theory that justifies this development. I am old enough to have known both the CEOs of 20 years ago and those of today. I can assure you that we CEOs of today are not 10 times better than those of 20 years ago.

What happened? Sadly, all too many members of the inner circle of the business elite participated in the over-expansion of executive compensation. It was justified by a claimed identity between the motivation of the executives and shareholder value. It is reasonably clear now that this theory has left a large number of poorer stockholders, especially including employee stockholders, not only unconvinced, but understandably disillusioned and angry.

The policy of vastly increasing executive compensation was also, at least with the brilliant vision of hindsight, terribly bad social policy and perhaps even bad morals.[6]

In individual cases the awards have been breathtakingly exorbitant. Pride of place here arguably goes to Disney former chairman and CEO Michael Eisner, whose pay packages often seemed to border on the realm of Disney-like fantasy. In 1997, for example, he earned more than the aggregate paychecks of the top 500 British CEOs as he exercised stock options worth more than $500 million. Many have questioned whether Disney's performance under Eisner's stewardship merited such largesse. Yet there has been no shortage of CEOs capable of giving Eisner a run for his money on this score. A notable case in point was Joseph Nacchio who, while CEO of telecoms group Qwest, took a pay package in 2001 potentially worth $194 million when the company posted a $4 billion loss and was busy firing employees. He clearly lacked a shame gene.

Then there is the phenomenon of "stealth" compensation relating to post-retirement pensions and perks. The most eye-catching retirement-to-grave security package was for Jack Welch, former chairman and CEO of General Electric. Among the revelations that emerged in the course of his divorce proceedings were lavish retirement benefits including a luxury New York apartment with servants, daily flower deliveries and wine, continuing use of the company jet and an $86,000 a year consultancy role on top of his generous pension.

FAILURE PAYS

Most damaging, in terms of corporate performance, have been pay packages that incorporate big pay-offs for failure, since they provide an incentive for incoming CEOs to take excessive risks in the knowledge that betting the corporate ranch carries no personal financial penalty. Once again Disney provides the most extraordinary example, with its $140m pay-off for failed president Michael Ovitz in the mid-1990s. He had been fired after just 14 months in the job. Fortunately for shareholders he had not been given the time or opportunity to bet the ranch.

In Europe boardroom pay awards have been less spectacular, but have, if anything, been more controversial, especially in countries with a strong egalitarian ethos. The grant of €60 million ($75m) of bonuses to Klaus Esser and other executives of Mannesmann after its takeover by British telecoms group Vodafone caused outrage in Germany and led to a criminal trial in which directors of the German conglomerate were accused of a breach of fiduciary duty. In the end the judge could see no grounds to pursue a criminal case against them, but she concluded that the men had broken corporate law in awarding, or abetting the award of, "inappropriate" bonuses.

At the time of writing, a further criminal case is under way. A similar row broke out in Sweden when it emerged that Percy Barnevik, the former chairman of the Swedish–Swiss engineering group ABB, had been granted an American-style stealth compensation package. And the final pay-off granted to Jean-Marie Messier, after he had brought Vivendi Universal close to bankruptcy, left French people aghast.

● Case study: Directors' Pay

STOCK OPTIONS FOR FREE

The extraordinary escalation in boardroom pay was closely associated with the growth of stock option awards. Effective lobbying by the Business Roundtable and other business groups prompted the US Financial Accounting Standards Board to retreat from a proposal to charge the cost of stock option awards as an expense in the profit and loss account. As a result many executives and even some shareholders came to regard stock options as free despite the fact that the cost to the company is real, being the amount the company gives up by not selling the option to an outside investor in the market. This led to the grant of stock options on such a lavish scale that the US shareholder activist Robert Monks dubbed it the greatest non-violent transfer of wealth from one class to another that history had ever seen.

This was a huge governance failure. Nowhere is the conflict of interest between principal and agent greater than in the area of boardroom pay. Yet non-executive directors on compensation committees – often other CEOs appointed on a friendly basis – have done little to restrain CEO pay and have fooled themselves into thinking that the grant of options helps align the interests of the CEO and the shareholders. Until recently, institutional shareholders made little protest at the dilution of their interest in the equity of the corporate sector. But when it comes to the ethical dimension of the problem there is a need for realism. To think that a stronger commitment to ethical values in corporations across the world could or would have curbed the boardroom pay spiral would be a pious hope. Nor are all executives necessarily being greedy and dishonest.

In the nature of things CEOs have strong egos and considerable self-belief. Like most of their fellow human beings they see their pay package as part of a scoring system that reflects on their performance and affects their sense of self-worth. The growth of a consultants' cottage industry researching boardroom pay comparisons has caused this scoring system to become more transparent. And when CEOs compare themselves with their peers they often feel that the compensation committee has failed fully to grasp the variety and depth of their talents. They naturally apply pressure for more.

For their part members of the compensation committee – who are not, of course, spending their own money – wish to be supportive of the CEO in driving the company forward, so they are reluctant to award below-average pay even if that is what the performance justifies. This leads to a well-intentioned but ill-judged "top quartile" syndrome. Usually transparency is the best means of regulating conflicts of interest. But in this case it has produced an upward ratchet in boardroom pay. Honest people are being trapped by this systemic flaw into granting excessive awards.

RISK AND REWARD

As for those in the New Economy where stock option awards in the larger companies appear to have gone way beyond the bounds of propriety, there are profound questions about what constitutes an equitable allocation of the rewards of enterprise between shareholders, executive directors and employees. This arises because human capital is a vital key to competitive advantage in this area. In the view of 19th-century economic liberals, directors owed their duty primarily to shareholders, who were entitled to the residual profits of enterprise after the claims of other stakeholders – customers, employees, suppliers, the community and the state – had been met. Investors were seen as the ultimate risk takers in the capitalist system.

From an economic perspective the idea was logical in an age when financial capital was scarce and labour was cheap and plentiful. Even allowing for the inequalities that prevailed in Europe and North America in the early stages of industrialisation, there was a certain legitimacy to this way of dividing the spoils of capitalism. As the sociologist Ernest Gellner noted, the individual capitalist was face to face with nature and those who returned with greater booty wrested from nature could claim legitimacy by virtue of their very visible contribution to the greater economic good. Yet today few entrepreneurs are face to face with nature and the capital in most quoted companies is at fifth or fiftieth hand. Innovation, as Gellner put it, is carried out on the shoulders of countless others. It is dependent on a shared scientific and technological culture to which many have contributed.

In the 21st century savings are no longer scarce as evidenced by the ease with which the United States, UK and Australia have been able to fund large deficits on their external accounts. Finance capital is a mere commodity, while human capital – skills acquired through education or experience at work – is scarce. And human capital belongs not to the company, but to the employees. Some human capital may be specific to the company. Or it may be transferable from one company to another. The outcome is that it becomes difficult to measure the value of the inputs of managers and employees, as against outside shareholders. The property rights in this kind of business become indistinct.

In such a world, which operates more on the basis of horizontal networks than a vertical hierarchy, it becomes harder to establish clear accountability. And there is a problem of legitimacy. Since so many big high-tech companies are cash rich – Microsoft being the most obvious case in point – they do not need to turn to outside shareholders for capital. While they would not have come into existence without the contribution of equity from outside shareholders at an early stage, that fact tends to be remote in the perceptions of many directors and employees. They do not see what the outside shareholders bring to the party. And they do not see those shareholders as the ultimate risk takers of the system since nowadays the risks are diversified across big institutional portfolios. In purely practical terms, the employees, and sometimes even the suppliers, are more heavily exposed to risk than shareholders.

The problem is compounded because there is no straightforward way to establish how profits should be shared between outside shareholders, directors and employees when it is impossible to identify a market value for the most creative individuals in the company or put a market value on the company-specific investment that individuals have made. In the circumstances it is not entirely surprising that people in the New Economy vastly increased their take, via stock option awards, at the outside shareholders' expense during the high-tech bubble that came to an end in 2000.[7]

THE MORALITY QUESTION

That does not mean that ethics are a mere side issue. As William McDonough implied in his Trinity Church address, the huge increase in the disparity between boardroom pay and the pay of the workforce raises questions of morality. And morality here, as so often, goes hand in hand with profitable business and good reputation. Where the inequality is blatant and rewards are clearly not justified by executives' performance, the workforce becomes demoralised. When the same phenomenon is replicated across the whole economy, the legitimacy of wealth creation is called into question. Much the same applies where a company has been involved in high-profile accidents involving pollution or loss of life. Awarding bonuses purely on the basis of financial performance in such circumstances can cause substantial reputational damage.

It is worth noting, too, that ethical issues arise in relation to the grant of stock options to employees. Many of the recipients are in no position to have a significant personal impact on the performance of the company or its share price. In effect, top management and boards of directors have presided over a paternalistic handout, encouraged by the false notion that such largesse is cost free. This may be bad economics, especially where the value of the option to a risk-averse employee is less than its cost. And it is arguably unethical, for when a company awards options in lieu of cash, it is borrowing from employees, receiving employment services today in exchange for variable and unpredictable payments in the future which often turn out to be non-existent. This is unfair to those employees who have little understanding of the stock market or the risks inherent in options.

MICROSOFT SAYS NO

Even before they were required to expense stock options under a proposed revision to the US accounting standard on stock options, some leading US companies concluded that options were a poor way of incentivising employees and that plain equity was better. Microsoft's CFO John Connors put the case against options very clearly:

The options program was originally designed to give employees enough money for retirement or a vacation home or to pay for their kids' education – goals that usually take 15 or 20 or 25 years to achieve. Yet because of the stock market's performance, people were making enough money to send 3,000 kids to college or build 30 vacation homes. Then the bubble burst, our stock declined by half, and roughly half our employees had loads of money but were sitting in the same offices and doing the same jobs as the other half, who would likely earn nothing from their options.

It was the worst of all possible worlds. At the same time, we were diluting the heck out of shareholders, who were telling us loud and clear that we should rethink the long term value proposition of our options program. Of course, shareholders hadn't paid much attention to that dilution when it was outstripped by growth, but when growth lags behind and expectations change, that dilution looks a lot different.[8]

It follows from all this that CEOs and those who sit on compensation committees should ask themselves whether the boardroom pay awards they are contemplating could damage workforce morale or adversely affect perceptions of the company in the community at large. They should also ask whether pay packages go beyond (or fall short of) what is required to attract, motivate and retain executives, instead of accepting wholesale the advice of the tame, conflicted pay consultant who is often appointed by the CEO rather than the compensation committee, knows what the CEO wants and will earn a handsome fee for delivering it. And they should ask themselves whether awarding options to the workforce at large is an appropriate means of payment. If they conclude that it is, they should follow by asking themselves whether they have done enough to inform employees of the nature of the risk in this form of award.

If a flawed compensation committee system throws up rewards that are manifestly overgenerous in relation to performance, it is of course open to executives to turn down bonuses or other parts of the overall compensation package.

This is not unusual in countries with a strong consensual industrial relations tradition such as Germany, where management board members sometimes surrender part of their salary to show solidarity with rank and file employees when radical cost-cutting measures cause redundancies.

While the pay consultants have done their best to create the illusion that boardroom pay determination approximates to a market-based system, the reality involves a high degree of discretion on the part of compensation committees and managers. So while it would be foolish to assume that moral conscience will dramatically change the overall boardroom pay picture, there will always be room for individuals to ask questions and to exercise moral judgement when making the key decisions.

● Case study:
OPTIONS BACKDATING AND SPRINGLOADING

The increasing use of stock options from the mid-1990s played an important part in the exponential rise in executive compensation in the United States. Yet only in 2006 did it emerge that the process whereby options were granted to executives had often been legally or ethically dubious. Scores of companies suddenly found themselves under investigation by the Securities and Exchange Commission. The high-tech sector was particularly affected, with even such respected giants as Apple being caught up in the saga.

Executive stock options give the executive the right to buy the company's stock at a set point in the future. The exercise (or strike) price is usually set at or near the stock price at the time the option is granted. What prompted the scandals was the manipulation of the exercise price.

The focus of concern in the rash of press headlines lay in two main areas. The first was options backdating, whereby companies issued options to the executives and backdated the date of their grant to a day when the company's stock was at its lowest recent point. As a result the executives enjoyed the right to buy the company's shares more cheaply and ended up owning options that were more valuable at the time of issue because the exercise price was below the stock price. In finance speak, the options were almost immediately "in the money".

Backdating to take advantage of past share price movements is usually illegal in the absence of adequate disclosure. And because the Sarbanes-Oxley Act introduced a requirement for swifter disclosure of the grant of options, backdating had anyway become less common by the time the scandals erupted in 2006. A tricky ethical issue also arose in relation to so-called springloading, in which the company issues stock options to executives just before an announcement that is likely to have a favourable impact on the stock price. A typical example of this forward-looking form of manipulation would arise where, say, a pharmaceutical company gains regulatory approval for a new drug. With a springloaded option, the exercise price reflects the stock price before the good news announcement. When the announcement comes and the stock price appreciates, the option immediately becomes more valuable. In effect, the option, now "in the money", has been granted to executives at a big discount.

INSIDE INFORMATION

By any common-sense definition this is insider trading. Yet springloading is not caught under the SEC's rules on insider trading because the grant of an option is not regarded as a purchase or sale transaction. Ethical questions nonetheless arise because executives are using privileged information for their own advantage before revealing that information to the market. There is also the question of whether outside shareholders' equity is being diluted.

SEC commissioner Paul Atkins has defended the practice, arguing that it does not amount to insider trading because no one is harmed. Speaking to a sceptical audience of institutional investors at the International Corporate Governance Network annual conference in Washington DC in July 2006 he suggested that springloading even provided benefits to shareholders because fewer stock options had to be issued to deliver a given reward to executives. In other words, the rest of the executives' overall pay package could be reduced to compensate for the uplift in the value of the springloaded options.

This can only be described as astonishingly naïve. The explosive growth in the use of stock options since the 1990s came without reductions in other forms of pay. Hence the extraordinary rise in inequality between executive pay and the average pay of the workforce. The notion that executives would

● Case study: Options Backdating and Springloading

suddenly start to exercise restraint with springloaded options when no restraint has been exercised over the issue of options more generally beggars belief.

JUST A HANDOUT

Moreover, it is open to question whether springloading achieves a good alignment of interests between management and shareholders. Since executive stock options usually are not exercisable for three years or more, granting options at a de facto discount may help in retaining good executives. Indeed, the intense competition for skilled employees in areas such as information technology provides the most plausible explanation for the widespread use of backdating and springloading. Yet if the options are large in relation to executives' overall assets, they might in theory become more risk averse in the hope of hanging on to the discount created by springloading. In practice, though, this is unlikely because executives know that options are a capricious and highly leveraged form of reward. The price responds to outside events that have nothing to do with the performance of the company. The reality is that springloading is just a handout to executives at shareholders' expense, which may or may not retain its value until the option is exercised.

In our view the practice is unethical, as is backdating. And since most executives see no reason to declare the value of the de facto discount to the Internal Revenue Service as part of their income, an ethical question arises, too, about tax evasion.

NOTES

1 *The Modern Corporation and Private Property*, by Adolph Berle and Gardiner Means (Macmillan, 1932).

2 Quoted in the Global Proxywatch newsletter, (6 May 2005).

3 *Back Door Links between Directors and Executive Compensation*, by David F. Larcker, Scott A. Richardson, Irem Tuna and Andrew J. Seary. For a summary, see <http://knowledge.wharton.upenn.edu/article/1189.cfm>.

4 For a full account, see *Charity Begins at the Board: Just Ask A. I. G.*, by Gretchen Morgenson, *New York Times*, (10 April 2005).

5 Speech for the Institute of Chartered Secretaries (August 2002).

6 Remarks at Trinity Church commemoration service (11 September 2002).

7 For a fuller discussion of this issue, see John Plender's *Going Off the Rails: Global Capital and the Crisis of Legitimacy*, chapter 11 (John Wiley, 2003).

8 From an interview in *The McKinsey Quarterly* (2005, No. 1).

Chapter 10

BANKERS & ADVISERS

SPEED-READ SUMMARY

- During economic good times when many are making money, the more dubious banking practices are often excused and regulatory rules are stretched. When the inevitable turnaround comes, these practices are laid bare and looked upon in a different light.

- The use of legal instruments to obtain retribution for ethical abuses can lead to the view that all wayward bankers needed to have done was to stay within the letter of the law. But this misses the point. At the time bankers often believed they were operating within the letter of the law. But they also had reasons to believe that, ethically, they were on thin ice.

- A combination of regulatory and technological change has created competitive pressures that have altered the nature of banking. Today, many banks opt to earn fatter fees for originating and structuring loans, rather than the slimmer spreads available for carrying loans on their balance sheet. This has changed the nature of ethical abuses in banks.

- Because these changes have been relatively recent, case studies are limited. In this chapter we focus in our examples of ethical dilemmas for J. P. Morgan Chase and Enron. It is our intention to say something about the dilemmas all bankers, treasurers and risk managers face and not something particular about these institutions.

The Enron story is so fascinating because Ken Lay, Jeff Skilling, and Andy Fastow are as Joseph Conrad put it – "one of us". The financial world really does have all the seductive charm that Oliver Stone's movie Wall Street *so graphically portrays and it is easy to see how flawed, normal human beings could not only be slowly and completely corrupted, but also be so oblivious to the entire process. I have no doubt that the lead actors of this tragedy are convinced of their own innocence.*[1]

Though we would have picked a different set of characters than Messrs Lay, Skilling and Fastow to make the point, this comment above by Ross Miller and Peter Fusaro relates to one of the assertions of this book, namely that there are crooks out there, and some of them were no doubt employed by Enron, but many of the people who get tangled up in ethical abuses seldom set out to do so.[2] Instead, they slip and slide until they find themselves in the middle of an ethical quagmire. Some of them are as surprised about where they have ended up as the rest of us. To quote an African proverb, do not look where you fall, but where you slipped.

While press reports are divided about the late Kenneth Lay, they suggest that Mr Skilling and Mr Fastow were more vulnerable to getting ethically lost than others. But there are some important aspects of the Enron case for bankers to mull over before urban mythology takes over and everyone concludes these were unusual men brought together in unusual times and that it couldn't happen again or to them. Our reading of the circumstances and incentives suggests to us, in the words of the ethically questionable UK National Lottery advert, "it could be you".

The rules change when markets crash, but the ethics don't.

It is important to note that a few years before Lay, Skilling and Fastow were vilified in the courtroom they were hailed as corporate heroes. For six years up to 2001 (the year of bankruptcy) Enron was named as *Fortune* magazine's "Most Innovative Company". Between 1985 and 2000, a number of innovations led to a relatively unknown energy company, Houston National Energy, to merge and later, as Enron, to grow into one of the world's largest companies by market capitalisation. Awards for innovation from the business press, bankers and investors do not encourage circumspection by management. Rather, it lulled Enron's managers into the belief that they were truly "masters of the universe", able to conjure up financial returns for everyone and deserving of a sizeable share of those returns for employing their brilliance. At Enron's *fin de siècle*, it resembled a den of thieves, but it was a den furnished with investor and press accolades. It should not be forgotten that with the exception of the odd short-seller, right up to the eve of its collapse, bankers, investors, employees and journalists scrambled to increase their exposure to this time bomb.

Moreover, contrary to popular folklore, Enron slid into bankruptcy not as a result of the illegality of the actions of the three gentlemen above, but as a result of a bad call on the markets and a hubristic risk-management system. The market risks they took made it likely that they would come unstuck at some point; but if they had been luckier with the prices of Californian gas, digital bandwidth, water and with the developments at their LNG power plant in Dabhol, India, they might have avoided bankruptcy in 2001 and their activities might not have come under the same scrutiny as they did. This is not as far-fetched as it seems. If energy and Indian stock prices had been in 2001 closer to their levels in 2005, Enron might have survived. Perhaps they would have been feted as corporate geniuses today. Messrs Lay, Skilling and Fastow might have avoided their current fate. The ethics of their behaviour and those of their bankers would of course be the same.

THE FALL-OUT FROM ENRON

It is also important to consider that the settlements forced on Enron's main bankers for the accusation of aiding and abetting fraud at Enron may have had more to do with the retributive desire of regulators and prosecutors to find someone to pay for the consequences of Enron's bankruptcy than with a strict reading of the law. Which is perhaps one reason why the regulatory agencies agreed to settle out of court with the bankers and analysts rather than to proceed with a court case, as they did with Enron's management. The consequences of Enron's bankruptcy were indeed substantial: a loss of $60 billion of shareholder value, worthless pension funds for 11,000 employees, lost jobs for 4,500 workers and a severe loss of credibility in American capitalism that led to the hurried passing of the Sarbanes-Oxley Act.

One of the lessons for market participants from the treatment of Enron, a lesson learned and forgotten in 1929–1932, is that when markets are booming and almost everyone involved is making hay, no one thinks too much about the ethically doubtful practices that some bankers undertake in order to win more business. Let us not make out that everyone is "on the game". No one sanctions illegal behaviour, but it is accepted that bankers are playing a game to see how much they can push at the edges of the law without infringing its letter. When the markets crash, the interpretations of the laws change.

Amid the rubble of a financial crash, there are plenty of people nursing hurts and losses and they want compensation, retribution or at least a scapegoat. The courts and politicians are not in the mood to be sympathetic to banks. The ethically dubious practices and occasions of banking gluttony that were known, but overlooked when everyone was making money, are seized upon as evidence of widespread theft. Dispassionate expert readings of the cases would consider that, on average, the interpretation of the regulations and laws are stretched against the bankers in the complaints. But the mood of the politicians and juries at the time is such that the courts are to be avoided. Regulators skilfully used this advantage to threaten and embarrass a few players into large out-of-court settlements in return for the regulators drawing a line in the sand that preserved businesses and industry. This action is often swiftly followed by announcements of changes in the law to make those questionable practices illegal. Yesterday's ethical code becomes today's laws. This pattern was clearly visible in 1930–1932, 2002–2004 and on other occasions in between.

It should be noted that one of the consequences of the unravelling of large "bezzles" is that lawmakers are often so shocked that it could have happened and so want to be seen to be doing something about it, that they tend to rush new legislation to stop it happening again. It is rare for laws made in haste to be well-judged and proportionate responses to the real problems. One other problem with yesterday's ethics becoming today's laws is that when memories begin to fade, the lasting impression is that all the bankers needed to have done then and today is to follow the letter of the law. At the time however the legal issues are often – though by no means always – less clear. Bankers should understand that legal interpretations of their actions may change depending on whether the markets are in boom or bust.

The ethical questions however do not change, and this may be a better compass to use in determining where they are going. To illustrate this we will look at an important part of the Enron imbroglio: an area where the bankers were accused of wrongdoing where, to us anyway, the legalities were less clear-cut, but the ethical behaviour was more clearly wrong. This is the area of "pre-pays" (which are essentially a futures contract where you pay today for the delivery of a commodity in the future) and the relationship between Enron and a special purpose entity called Mahonia. This is not to say that Enron, with the support of its bankers, did nothing illegal. For our purposes, however, it is in the individual actions and legally grey areas that market participants need most help when assessing their ethical responsibilities.

THE CHANGING FACE OF BANKING

To understand the issues more fully, a little background on the changing landscape of banking is necessary. Banking has changed substantially in recent decades in response to technological and regulatory changes. To some extent banks are part of the information industry in that they put lenders in touch with borrowers. If the lenders had perfect information on who and where the appropriate borrowers were and were able to structure and manage their risks themselves, they would not need banks. Something similar could be said of borrowers. Consequently, the collapse of information costs has dramatically changed banking.

Large companies can now go directly to the securities markets to raise funds. At the same time, regulators, credit rating agencies and risk managers have required banks to set aside increasing amounts of expensive capital for the risks they take on to their balance sheet. Consequently, banks are increasingly forgoing putting loans on their balance sheets; instead, they originate and structure loans. The corporate bond markets and associated credit derivative markets have grown dramatically since 1990 and a large proportion of this growth is represented by securitised mortgages and packages of loans that would previously have resided on bank balance sheets.

The Enron imbroglio also happened against a background of very low interest rates from the end of 1998 to Enron's bankruptcy in 2002. The interest rate regime originated in part from the collapse in October 1998 of the hedge fund, Long-Term Capital Management.[3] In a gamble for redemption, the managers had increased their leverage substantially and in the subsequent near-collapse there were real fears that the financial system would temporarily cease to function, thereby spreading the dislocation. These fears appear overblown today, but at the time they seemed real. The fear was partly fuelled by the previous 12 months of financial stress amid the Asian financial crisis and dramatic movements in the dollar/yen foreign exchange market. In response, the Federal Reserve pumped liquidity into the financial system and cut interest rates.

With money so cheap to borrow, companies that were flush with cash and creative accountants would have come across plenty of opportunities to leverage those cash flows. On the other side, with interest rates low, bankers were making little money from loans and were eager to earn fees for originating and structuring loans. Along came Enron with a finance team lauded by the financial press for its innovation. It was a banker's dream ticket. Mahonia was born in this context. It was useful to note that while high interest rates are often seen as usurious and unethical, low interest rates can be a front for unethical behaviour too.

● Case study:
MAHONIA

In this case study we do not intend to scrutinise Enron's bankruptcy from every angle, but to examine a specific area which throws up some of the tension between the law and ethics. Transactions between Mahonia, Enron and J. P. Morgan Chase were the subject of much legal argument after the event.[4] We believe that paying more attention to the ethics of the issue would have given the perpetrators a better steer as to how the lawyers would consider the transaction at a future date. The main source of the material used in this discussion is the US Securities and Exchange Commission. We offer no new information but perhaps some different insights.

Mahonia is the collective name given to two special purpose entities called Mahonia Limited and Mahonia Natural Gas Limited. Mahonia was presented as the "third party" in transactions where the other parties were Enron and J. P. Morgan Chase, one of the group's main bankers. Forward contracts, where there is a payment today for a delivery of something tomorrow, are as old as the hills. They are critical to supplying the liquidity for economic activity. In a forward contract, Enron would get paid today for committing to supply a fixed amount of a commodity every month for one year to, in this case, Mahonia. Enron was getting the use of cash before it had delivered any product and so part of the value of this forward contract is the time value of money (the value of having money today versus tomorrow) which is effectively the cost of a 12-month loan to Enron.

The key point is that although this is a commodity futures contract, it is possible to break it down into its component parts, and to hedge all of the parts except for the time value of money. The component that is left looks and feels like a loan, but is not called one. This is what Enron did through a series of transactions. Commodity price risk was first transferred from Enron to Mahonia and then from Mahonia to Chase and finally from Chase back to Enron. The net effect was that Chase and Mahonia had fees for shuffling commodity risk around and Enron had something which resembled a loan from Chase.

The prosecutors alleged that Enron's intention was to obtain a loan and that this was a subterfuge to keep the loan off its balance sheet. But deriving a loan from a commodity transaction by itself is neither unusual nor illegal. It is how many commodity trading houses fund their trading operations and it is the cornerstone of many Islamic banking products. What was the intention of Enron's officers? The intention was not to loot the company – not directly anyway. If it were, they would have done it differently. The use of these transactions allowed Enron to leverage its constant and strong presence in the (energy-related) commodity markets to derive very flexible cash flows that could be tailored to many purposes from the smoothing of payments, hedging of liabilities and speculation of energy markets. Enron used them to produce liquidity in a mirror image to valuation changes of its illiquid assets, chief among these being the LNG power plant in Dabhol, India and broadband and cable infrastructure in the US. In effect, Enron transferred the liquidity it could access in the commodity markets to its portfolio of illiquid assets. This looked good when valuations of these illiquid assets were rising and as a result Enron's share price rose.

There is some sense to this type of transaction if it is modest in scale and backed by safe, long-term, if illiquid, assets. However, because Enron's officers were paid in stock options and because the external stock analysts did not fully understand what they were doing, Enron's officers found that they could raise the value of the stock, make a lot of money and look like clever heroes by doing more of these types of transactions. Indeed, they had an incentive to do more of these transactions than they had safe long-term assets to do them with. The incentives were not all financial. They were being feted as geniuses – a word with an unfortunate history of usage in financial markets. They began to believe what they read in the business press. They further believed that they could take more risks because they were so clever and had so much access to liquidity that they could come up with a solution if things began to go wrong. And so they began adding Enron stock (not a safe, long-term asset) as the collateral.

At the root of the problem, in our view, was not so much that Enron and their bankers were creating loans out of commodities trading and not putting them on their balance sheet – the bankers could reasonably have thought this was legal if the lawyers and auditors said it was so. The root of the problem was that the banks created structures that conflicted with Enron's officers and incentivised them to make poor risk-management decisions that were invisible to wider scrutiny. It should be noted that if Mahonia had a set of trustees not remunerated through Enron stock, and if they were advised by an independent auditing company how to mark-to-market Enron's assets so as to determine the size of the pre-pays, these transactions would have been legal and ethical. But they would probably also have been far smaller, more transparent and, as a result, they would have earned smaller fees.

One of the associated costs of a company's breakdown in ethical standards

● Case study: Mahonia

is that individual greed begins to permeate everything. In Enron's case it
moved ethically questionable activities across the line into illegal ones.
There was nothing about the intention of the transactions that required
Mahonia to have been effectively controlled and directed by J. P. Morgan
Chase and for Andy Fastow, Enron's CFO, and his wife to be part owners of
the special purpose entities and vehicles that carried out the transactions
with Mahonia. But keeping it "in house" meant that there were fewer
constraints and more fees to share among those who were driving these
transactions. Strip away the unnecessary greed and look at the underlying
transactions and they could have been made legal.

Prosecution lawyers made a great deal of the fact that the bankers
considered that these transactions were in essence loans. Yet there are few
financial transactions with a futures component that cannot be viewed as a
loan of some kind. These financial niceties of course would not convince a
jury baying for blood in the aftermath of the lost jobs, lost pensions and
lost investments of the Enron collapse. Using liquidity from commodity-
related transactions to liquefy less liquid assets, is innovative and leans
against accounting rules. The bankers could say that if external accountants
had agreed to the way the transactions were accounted for, and if
everything that should be disclosed to the analysts and credit rating
agencies was being disclosed, and the independent board members had
sanctioned the share options and establishment of the SPVs, then they were
not without justification in considering what they did was within legal
limits. But whatever the legalities, the bankers had a duty of care to the
company that was not properly carried out. Among the questions they
should have asked themselves to have avoided the business and to have
saved them a great deal including some large fines are as follows:

➤ ETHICAL QUESTIONS FOR BANKERS

1.   Am I devolving ethical responsibility to others?

The first line of defence of a company against management abuse is
the board of directors. Enron's board was a powerful set of well-
qualified individuals. Next in line were the auditors, especially given
that the issue in Enron's case was not so much the transactions
themselves, but the appropriate accounting treatment. After the
auditors you may consider that the analysts and credit rating   ➤

agencies should have had a more restraining influence on Enron in its request to the bankers to create these structures and transactions. It would appear that the bankers at J. P. Morgan Chase thought that if the lawyers and accountants were happy, then who were they to question? However, as we repeatedly argue throughout this book, ethics are not things we can hang up in the front cloakroom of the bank or pass on to others. We carry them with us at all times. This is all the more the case when bankers are not passively responding to a request from a client, but take an active role in recommending and structuring transactions, as they did in the case of Enron.

2. Are there disguised conflicts of interest in the transaction?

What immediately comes to mind in regard to Enron is that the chief financial officer, Andy Fastow, and his wife were beneficiaries of some of the SPVs that entered into transactions with Enron. It could be argued that in these transactions his interests were largely aligned with those of Enron's shareholders in that they served to boost Enron's shareholder value. Importantly, the fact that Enron had entered into transactions with "related parties" was disclosed and had board approval. However, Mr Fastow benefited from the size of the transactions in fees rather than sharing in their risks and so he was in personal conflict when deciding, with his Enron CFO hat on, the size of the risks Enron should be exposed to, via transactions with SPVs which he was party to. The size of these fees to Mr Fastow from the SPVs was not fully disclosed. While more subtle than commonly thought, there were indeed disguised conflicts in these transactions that the bankers could have seen and that in certain cases raised a number of legal issues.

3. Have I contrived a situation, or been party to the contrivance, which puts counterparties to a transaction at a disadvantage to myself or my partners?

In the case of Enron, the contrivance was not so much the transactions but their governance, which created an incentive for the risks to the company to be disregarded.

4. Will this transaction cause unmitigated harm to anyone?

Should the bankers, often involved in small parts of the overall operation of the company, have anticipated that the poor risk ➤

management and implicit leverage of Enron's transactions would inevitably harm Enron's shareholders, pensioners and employees? Should the bankers have cried wolf when the shareholders were rejoicing in the creativity of Enron's management and its bankers? One way in which the bankers could have mitigated the potential harm was to have made it very clear to their client and to the client's board, the circumstances in which the liquidity of the company would be threatened under these new structures and how the sensitivity of its exposure had been changed by these structures. They could have presented a scenario or stress test. Doing so, would also have addressed any concerns they may have had about the contrivance of these transactions.

● Case study:
McKINSEY

For many firms a statement of mission and values is essentially a public relations document. The board and top management make little effort to ensure that the values are embedded in the culture of the organisation. At McKinsey, the world's pre-eminent management consultancy firm, the values really do matter. They are little different today from when Marvin Bower took charge in the 1930s of a near-bankrupt accountancy and engineering firm and started turning it into the leading practitioner in top management consulting that McKinsey subsequently became.

Firms that place emphasis on fostering an ethical culture often owe this commitment to the powerful vision of a forceful founder. That is certainly true of McKinsey and Marvin Bower, who believed strongly in the importance of a shared institutional personality. In 1974 he wrote:

Any group of people that works together for years develops a philosophy, a tradition, a set of common values. One of the highest achievements in leadership is the ability to shape those values in a way that builds successful institutions. At its most practical level, the benefit of a managed value system is that it guides the actions of our people at all levels and in every part of our widespread empire; therefore, it permits greater self-control and self-governance. In a profession where service is all we offer, and where the majority of our professionals are relatively new, a strong culture that guides individual action is crucial. Our heritage [is] the ideas that have always guided our destiny.[5]

LIVING THE VALUES

Today McKinsey partners would probably not refer to the McKinsey "empire", but all McKinsey firm members are required to absorb a document called *A Guide to Living our Values,* which substantially reflects the Bower philosophy. Some of the values are standard injunctions for professional advisory and services businesses, such as the need to put client interests ahead of the firm's and to maintain independence and objectivity in taking positions that are in the client company's best interest as opposed to what firm members would like to hear. Other values are distinctive, most notably the obligation on every member of the firm to dissent where he or she feels that something is unsound or not in the best interests of the client or the firm. That is an obligation, not a right. Discussion of values is embedded at all levels of the firm, as are conversations about how best to serve the client's interests. McKinsey people are expected to question and challenge each other in the normal course of doing the job. This contributes to a non-hierarchical, inclusive ethos, as well as making the firm an exciting place for people to work, although the conversations are arduous and can make for slow decision making.

A feature of McKinsey's values that differentiates it from many law firms and the accountancy based professional firms is that it operates as one firm with a single balance sheet and operating statement. There is no profit and loss account for individual partners and no pressure to meet numbers. What matters in the firm is giving the best possible service to the client. In reviews of individual performance, adherence to the firm's values, including the obligation to dissent, is an important criterion. The aim is to foster a spirit of partnership with an emphasis on teamwork, trust and transparency. The advantage of the "one firm" approach is that it minimises the scope for conflicts of interest. Whenever McKinsey was presented with opportunities to diversify into a broader range of services, Bower managed to persuade his partners not to dilute the focus of the firm. The clients are owned by the firm, not by a particular office, practice or sector.

TAKING THE PAIN

Under Bower, integrity was paramount. "If you are not willing to take pain to live by your principles," he once remarked, "there is no point in having principles." Bower's biographer, Elizabeth Haas Edersheim, records a remarkable instance of how the partnership took pain when its values were violated, quoting Chuck Ames, a retired chairman of Acme Cleveland and former McKinsey alumnus:

The best performing associate in the office was Gerry Andlinger. He was very smart and viewed as key. He was working with Stromberg Carlson on a top management organization study. He had recommended an organization change and the creation of a new officer's position, and recommended himself for the position. I don't think he recommended himself in writing, but in discussions with the client he recommended himself for that job. He was doing work for Dawes Bibby who was a good friend of Marvin's. [Dawes] called Marvin… and told him what had happened. Marvin said, 'You have 30 minutes to clear out. You're all done. And if you need some help, I'll be glad to get the building services to help you get your things out, but you're out.' That was it.

Gerry was clearly the smartest, if not one of the two or three smartest guys in the firm. He was a real loss to the firm, but that didn't make any difference to Marvin. His position was that you live by these principles or you're out of here. Marvin made a point of communicating that what Gerry did is not how we run the firm. I think this was on a Friday, and Gerry had a dinner party that night. My wife and I were there. I said. 'Gerry, I'm sorry to hear about this' Gerry said, 'No, he did the right thing. I violated principles, I got caught, it's the right thing – throw me out.'

Among other things, Marvin Bower's response to this violation of the principle of independence and objectivity sent a very powerful signal to everyone in the firm about the centrality of the values it claimed to adhere to.

THE DOTCOM TEST

Yet maintaining the old values has become much harder as the firm has turned into a global organisation. And as with so many other firms, McKinsey's values were severely tested during the dotcom boom of the 1990s. When Enron crashed the firm came under a harsh spotlight. Jeffrey Skilling, the CEO, had been one of McKinsey's brightest people and had moved to Enron after consulting for the energy company when it began its transformation from an unexciting utility into a fast-growing energy trader. McKinsey was an important architect of the strategic thinking that made Enron one of Wall Street's favourite companies. One prominent McKinsey partner even sat in on several board meetings. So when Enron collapsed there was inevitably a suspicion that the consultants might have turned a blind eye to the rottenness of the corporate culture. At the very least the world's pre-eminent consultancy firm had failed to detect the weakness of the Enron balance sheet or sense the flaws in its business model.

Overall, McKinsey did not read the dotcom boom well and during the period of market euphoria it abandoned Marvin Bower's philosophy on fees by permitting them to be linked to client performance. With fledgling dotcom companies it even took stock in lieu of fees. This raised questions about how to maintain objectivity and independence as the firm's fortunes became more closely tied to the financial fortunes of client companies. The problems were compounded because the firm overrecruited during the bubble. There followed much soul searching about whether it was right to dismiss people before they had had a chance to show their abilities. In the end people were dismissed, but senior partners chose to lose money, knowing that they could have cut more, and more quickly.

To its credit, the firm recognised in the new millennium that its values had become strained and it has worked hard to rebuild them. In June 2004 the partners organised a "values" day for the whole firm, in which people were asked to identify where the values were not being observed and what was going wrong. A great deal of the McKinsey top leadership's time was devoted to this exercise, even though it meant that less time was spent on the clients. The McKinsey leadership felt that the exercise was essential to reasserting the firm's identity.

McKinsey has always been a meritocracy and has an annual turnover among its consultants of about 15 per cent a year. But it likes to think it is a caring meritocracy and that those who are counselled to leave usually recognise that it is not the right place for their particular skills and aspirations. They tend to retain a deep affinity with the firm. Marvin Bower's precept that values should be instilled into newcomers by constant reiteration at every opportunity continues to be followed.

As with other global firms McKinsey faces a huge challenge in trying to embed a genuinely common culture across the world. In Asian countries such as Japan, China and South Korea the obligation to dissent can seem an alien form of behaviour that rubs uncomfortably against local behavioural norms. And for the Japanese, with a tradition of lifetime employment in large companies, the notion of shedding 15 per cent of the employees every year is deeply shocking. The potential problem for those who go is loss of face in a society where such a loss is greatly feared.

McKinsey has addressed these problems in Asia by giving outplacement help and by ensuring that no one can tell who has gone voluntarily and who was fired. Because many of the departed alumni have subsequently enjoyed successful careers, the risk of a stigma on leaving has become less threatening and the problem has become less pressing over time. Yet there remains a risk with such countries that the McKinsey culture has to coexist with a distinctive local culture.

BOWER'S CORE INSIGHTS

We believe that McKinsey's approach to ethics is one from which other firms can draw valuable lessons. Yet it is salutary to recall that one of Marvin Bower's core insights sits uneasily with the modern business ethos. Bower believed that while financial considerations cannot be ignored, business goals must not be financial. If they are, he argued, the business will fail to serve its customers and ultimately enjoy less profit. Since the shareholder value movement took root in the 1990s and the stock option culture became entrenched, the increasingly narrow interpretation placed on shareholder value by business people is simply not compatible with this commitment to non-financial goals. Yet if Bower's precept had not been so widely ignored, many of the corporate scandals at the turn of the millennium would not have happened. The conclusion must surely be that when the new ethos is so completely at odds with this profound insight of the founder and greatest luminary of the management consultancy profession, it is time for the ethos to change.

NOTES

1 Quotation from Peter C. Fusaro and Ross Miller, *What Went Wrong at Enron*, (John Wiley & Sons, 2002).

2 See Peter C. Fusaro and Ross Miller, *What Went Wrong at Enron*, (John Wiley & Sons, 2002).

3 See Roger Lowenstein, *When Genius Failed: the Rise and Fall of Long-Term Capital Management* (Random House: October 2001).

4 Prosecutors pursued Enron finance officials on counts of falsifying accounting information, but J. P. Morgan Chase and insurers who gave guarantees on transactions between J. P. Morgan, Mahonia and Enron reached a $600 million settlement, part of which includes the bank denying any wrong doing. Following the settlement J. P. Morgan CEO William Harrison said "We believe our firm acted appropriately on all transaction involving the insurance companies." This was reported in *BusinessWeek* on 8 January 2003.

5 Quoted in *McKinsey's Marvin Bower* by Elizabeth Haas Edersheim (John Wiley & Sons, 2004).

Chapter 11

AUDITORS

SPEED-READ SUMMARY

■ Independence and objectivity are vital qualities in auditors, who act as guarantors of the integrity of the numbers on which the capitalist system depends.

■ Any loss of independence weakens the accountability of management to shareholders and erodes trust in capital markets, which is what happened after the collapse of Enron and the demise of Andersen, its auditor.

■ There is endemic confusion, in auditing, over the identity of the client. In many jurisdictions the auditor is, in law, appointed by shareholders, but in practice auditors tend to regard company executives as the client.

■ The client identity problem is exacerbated by the big accountancy firms' change in business model. They have moved from being professional firms, in which auditing was the central function, to being growth-hungry multi-service conglomerates, in which conflicts of interest have become more acute.

■ Academic psychologists have found that auditors greatly overestimate their ability to manage conflicts of interest and are subject to unconscious biases when confronting difficult ethical dilemmas.

■ Attempts by lawmakers and regulators to address the erosion of the auditor's independence and remedy recent ethical lapses have had some impact, but the big accountancy firms' business model, with its tendency to treat management rather than shareholders as client, has not radically changed, especially outside the US.

Independence is a concept of fundamental importance in business relations and corporate governance. It is above all crucial in auditing, which provides a guarantee of the integrity of the numbers on which an efficient allocation of capital within the capital market system depends. The job of auditors is to express an independent opinion on whether financial statements are reliable and credible. They report on the statements' compliance with the law and accounting standards and, depending on the jurisdiction, whether the accounts prepared by the board reveal either a fair, or a true and fair, picture of economic reality. Unlike most other advisers auditors have an overwhelming public-interest obligation, which has been put with great clarity by the former US Chief Justice Warren Burger:

By certifying the public reports that collectively depict a corporation's financial status, the independent auditor assumes a public responsibility transcending any employment relationship with the client. The independent public accountant performing this special function owes ultimate allegiance to the corporation's creditors and stockholders, as well as to the investing public. This "public watchdog" function demands that the accountant maintain total independence from the client at all times and requires complete fidelity to the public trust.[1]

Very importantly, auditors play a central part in policing the conflict of interest implicit in the principal–agent relationship between shareholders and management. If they allow their independence to be compromised, a decline in the quality of audits will cause the chain of accountability from management to shareholders to go slack, trust in capital markets to erode and the cost of capital to increase as a result. This is precisely what happened in the period of falling ethical standards at the turn of the millennium.

Auditors and other professionals frequently refer to independence as a habit of mind. Yet this definition is less than adequate. Independence is better regarded as a freedom from business relationships, institutional structures and incentives that impair objectivity. It is not enough for professionals themselves to be satisfied that they are independent. Those with a genuine professional and ethical commitment should aspire to a freedom from compromising business environments and relationships that would satisfy a reasonable and well-informed third party that their objectivity was unimpaired.

THREATS TO OBJECTIVITY

Auditors have always faced problems with independence. If they own shares in the company they audit, for example, or if the audit client represents a disproportionately large share of the accountancy firm's fee income, objectivity is likely to be eroded. Because it is hard to do the job without establishing good working relations with the executives in the finance and accounting areas of the client company, there is inevitably a risk that the relationship will become too cosy. That risk is further heightened where the audit partner is invited to join the client company as chief financial officer or in any other role where there will be contact with the auditors.

While the accountancy profession and accountancy firms all have their own ethical rules and guidelines to deal with these potential impairments of objectivity and independence, there is always a risk that the rules may not keep pace with evolving business practice or fully cover the particular circumstances in which individual auditors find themselves. So auditors have to ask themselves key questions that go beyond mere compliance with professional and firm codes. The first one is whether anything in their business relationships, institutional environment or incentive arrangements puts at risk their independence, objectivity or integrity. A second, which concerns a fundamental ethical principle common to all advisory businesses, is whether the interests of the firm are being put above the interests of the client. Yet in the case of the auditor this question is complicated by continuing confusion over the identity of the real client.

In most developed countries the appointment and pay of the auditor has until recently in company law been a matter for shareholders to decide in the annual meeting. Yet in practice the auditor's job and pay have traditionally been in the gift of management. Managers do not have much incentive to encourage effective policing of their agency relationship with shareholders. Many feel anyway that their vision for the business is fully in alignment with the shareholders' interests. And in the 1960s and

1970s managers started to complain that the audit delivered little value to the company. Under pressure from corporate clients, who bargained fiercely to hold audit fees down when inflation was going up, the big accountancy firms thus changed their business model from one that focused on delivering quality audits for shareholders to a more commercially driven approach. The biggest firms turned themselves into global financial advisory conglomerates, providing management consulting, actuarial, human resource, legal and other services to their audit clients. Managers, who were only too happy to be cross-sold these new services, supplanted the shareholders as the auditor's real client.

As the firms' non-audit fee income grew very rapidly, auditing came to be perceived as a low-growth, unglamorous part of the business – an orphan product in a world where most employees wanted to work in the non-audit areas of the firm. Some firms refused to take on audit work unless audit clients offered them non-audit assignments, which carried the clear and ethically dubious message that it was uneconomic for them to do audit work without a cross-subsidy from other activities. The word low-balling, the practice of loss-leading with a low audit fee to win non-audit business, came into common parlance. This had important consequences for competition. It meant that cross-subsidised audit services were being offered below a price at which it was economic for smaller audit firms to come into the market. So this tended to entrench the dominance of the big firms in what many perceived to be an overconcentrated audit market.

BURGEONING CONFLICTS OF INTEREST

In this new world conflicts of interest multiplied. The problem was not limited to the audit/non-audit conflicts. The tax partners in accountancy firms, for example, became increasingly involved in mass marketing aggressive tax shelters, on which audit partners in the same firm would then have to pass an audit judgement, while profiting from the selling efforts of their fellow partners in the tax practice. Consultants installed financial information systems on which their fellow audit partners would have to reach an opinion in relation to the effectiveness of the system's internal controls which were fundamental to the integrity of the company's financial statements. And so on and so forth. Underlying it all was the basic point that the professional ethos was declining, as was the firms' ethical commitment. Rewards within partnerships, as in law firms, actuarial practices and other professional partnerships, were increasingly tailored to ensure that the biggest pay went to those who brought in most business. In the late 1990s at Ernst & Young, for example, some audit partners were given targets to meet for the sale of non-audit services to corporate clients. Failure to meet the target resulted in an automatic pay reduction of ten per cent.[2] This growth-hungry approach to incentives was perfectly designed to turn audit watchdogs into poodles. The independence of audit partners who presided over the low-growth part of the business was inevitably compromised.

The extent of the compromise emerged very clearly in the UK Department of Trade inspectors' report on the fraudulent business empire of Robert Maxwell, published in 2001. An internal memo sent by a senior partner in Coopers & Lybrand Deloitte (now subsumed into PricewaterhouseCoopers in the UK) outlined the firm's strategy towards the audit as follows:

The first requirement is to continue to be at the beck and call of RM [ie, Robert Maxwell], his sons and his staff, appear when wanted and provide whatever is requested.

In this case the role of the auditor had clearly degenerated into that of a lackey/poodle.

As the economist John Kay has argued, the auditors' position exemplifies the most famous problem in game theory, the Prisoner's Dilemma, in which rational crooks shop each other to their own ultimate disadvantage. In terms of the way the audit world works the dilemma arises because for a single firm in a respected profession, or an individual practitioner in a respected firm, the most profitable strategy is to benefit from the reputation for rigour and integrity established by others without contributing to it oneself. Since free riding is the most profitable strategy for everyone, reputations are inevitably eroded. Kay expands the point, saying:

The merit of competitive markets is satisfied customers and so it is with supervisory services. If property owners hire the police, policing strategies will suit property owners; if burglars hire the police, policing strategies will suit burglars. Since the audit process is one in which the property owners – the shareholders pay for the police and the potential burglars – the corporate executives – appoint them, we should expect scrutiny to be costly but not rigorous and frequently this is what we find.[3]

In the litigious environment of the US where lawsuits against auditors have multiplied, an important part of the story was that accounting standards became increasingly detailed, while there was a growing tendency to emphasise form over substance. Auditors sought to protect themselves from professional negligence claims by adopting a rule-checking approach instead of trying to arrive at a genuinely independent professional judgement on the fairness of the financial statements. In the stock market bubble of the late 1990s independence and ethics reached their lowest ebb. At Enron and WorldCom, the two most notorious corporate collapses of the period, Andersen took more non-audit fees than audit fees from these clients. Yet this fee imbalance was probably less important, in causing trouble, than the fact that its business model in both cases was fixated on keeping management happy in the interests of future fee generation for Andersen partners. Everyone lost sight, at the time, of the vital importance of the audit function for the integrity of the capital market system. The interests of the real audit clients, the shareholders, were neglected.

A final twist to the story of declining professional standards lay in the globalisation of the Big Five accountancy firms. PricewaterhouseCoopers, KPMG, Ernst & Young, Deloitte & Touche and Andersen used a common brandname across the world. The remaining four continue to do so. Yet the right to carry out a statutory audit in most jurisdictions is usually granted only to local firms. This means that the big global firms are really no more than loose confederations. They have franchised their brand names, but do not have full ability to enforce consistent audit quality across the world. And since they have all installed firewalls to ensure that legal liabilities for professional negligence cannot fall on partners in member firms in other countries, the chief external discipline for uniform global audit standards is weakened. The fragility of these loose confederations was exposed by the disintegration of Andersen after the Enron debacle. Each individual member firm of the Andersen global partnership rushed to hook up with the most attractive local partner of the Big Four in an unedifying *sauve qui peut* dash once it became clear that Andersen in the US would not survive.

In international institutions such as the World Bank which make use of the Big Four's audit services in developing countries, staff are highly critical of the uneven quality of the audits delivered by the Big Four. They feel that the firms have been selling their audit services on a false prospectus and question whether this approach, brilliantly successful in purely business terms, was professional or ethical. The point was graphically borne out when the Japanese arm of PricewaterhouseCoopers, ChuoAoyama PwC, was ordered by Japan's Financial Services Agency to suspend offering audit services to its bigger corporate clients for two months in 2006 for complicity in fraudulent accounting at Kanebo, a cosmetics company. This followed the arrest of three PwC auditors for, it was alleged, wilfully certifying false accounts at Kanebo for a period of five years. What emerged clearly from the affair was that audit standards at ChuoAoyama PwC were conspicuously lower than at the national firms of PwC in the US or parts of Europe. The global network had failed to impose common ethical or audit standards on a global basis.

THE ILLUSION OF OBJECTIVITY

How is it that partners and employees in audit firms continue to regard themselves as independent and objective when their profession has turned itself into a growth-hungry business where the institutional framework and incentive structures militate against objectivity? Much academic psychological research has been conducted into ethical lapses. The conclusions suggest that while most people have a realistic view of how others will behave in ethically challenging situations, everyone is wildly optimistic about their own behaviour.

There is exceptional overoptimism, it seems, in relation to the ability to remain uninfluenced by biases or conflicts of interest. Just as people tend to believe that they are better drivers than everyone else, they expect to act more ethically than everyone else. This leads to an illusion of objectivity whereby good people regularly engage in unethical behaviour without being aware of it because they over-rely on intuitive thinking or are influenced by unconscious bias.

Convincing evidence of this emerges in an experiment conducted by academic psychologists on 139 professional auditors.[4] Participants were given different auditing cases to examine, involving controversial areas of accounting such as revenue recognition or capitalisation versus expensing of expenditures (which was, incidentally, the issue on which the accountancy scandal at WorldCom turned). The auditors were told that the cases were independent of each other and were randomly assigned either to work for the company or to work for an outside investor considering investing in the company in question.

The psychologists found that the auditors who were told they were working directly for the company were 31 per cent more likely to accept the various dubious accounting treatments than those who were told they were working for outside investors. Other work by the same academics has demonstrated that while auditors were aware of the biasing influence of the particular role they fulfilled, they failed to grasp how powerful the bias was and were unable to correct for it. When these professional people were accountable to a partisan audience with clear preferences, they were found to be more willing to engage in actions consistent with the interests of their audience that they would otherwise find ethically problematic.[5]

SOME REMEDIES, BUT AN UNCHANGED BUSINESS MODEL

The Sarbanes-Oxley Act in the US and corporate governance codes in Europe have now tried to address the confusion over the identity of the audit client and the auditors' flawed business model by shifting responsibility for the appointment and pay of the auditor to audit committees peopled by independent non-executive directors. In many countries oversight has been strengthened and restrictions have been introduced in the provision of non-audit services to audit clients. It is becoming common for audit partners to be rotated at regular intervals, while in countries such as Italy the audit firm itself is rotated. Regulatory authorities such as the US Public Company Accounting Oversight Board are taking a close and healthy interest in the way audit partners are incentivised.

For their part the big accountancy firms are on their mettle since the raft of corporate collapses in the first half of the decade, the demise of Andersen and the US Department of Justice's investigation into the sale of aggressive tax shelters by KPMG. Audit has become less of an orphan business because it has been generating more money as a result of the Sarbanes-Oxley Act's demanding requirements, especially in relation to internal controls. Since the Act has extra-territorial reach, covering foreign companies listed in the US, the non-US members of the global accountancy partnerships are feeling additional benefit over and above increases in fees on the back of their own regulators' responses to domestic corporate scandals. Ethics partners are now normal in big accountancy firms, with a remit to ensure high standards are observed. The big firms have also produced statements of values to be applied globally, while efforts have been stepped up to achieve more consistent auditing standards worldwide. The professional bodies of the accountancy world likewise prescribe unvarying ethical standards globally.

Yet it remains to be seen whether the firms really can enforce global auditing standards and whether a common set of values can be embedded in the hugely different ethical and religious cultures that prevail in the countries where the firms operate. Arguing that a client should be turned away by the global partnership on ethical grounds entails big conflicts of interest when member firms stand to lose very different amounts of fee income that the client delivers to different firms in the global partnership. The conflict is then compounded because whatever the global values code may say, we all know that attitudes to ethics are highly variable from country to country.

The fact remains that the Big Four still aspire, outside the US at least, to be multi-service advisory conglomerates. Many of the leaders of the business whom we encounter tend to talk as though they do not see auditing as the key to future growth, which implies that there is a continuing question over the compatibility of the goals and incentive structures in the Big Four with genuine auditor independence. Nor is it our impression that they uniformly talk as though the business model has really changed. So for all the well-intentioned efforts of lawmakers, regulators and auditors to clean up the business since 2000, the Big Four and the wider accountancy profession have arguably yet to meet the test on the independence of the auditor of satisfying a reasonable and well-informed third party that objectivity is unimpaired.

> ## CONCLUDING QUESTIONS FOR PARTNERS IN PROFESSIONAL FIRMS

1. Are you aware of any threats to your independence, objectivity or integrity in your relations with clients? If so, what are you doing to mitigate them? Is the attempt to mitigate the problem diluted by concern for the bottom line?

2. Is your approach to the independence issue driven more by compliance with the stated rules of the firm or profession than by carefully considered judgement, informed by the rules, in the light of the individual circumstances?

3. Have you considered whether your judgement on ethical issues, notably on conflicts of interest, might be subject to unconscious bias?

4. In offering consultancy services to the audit client, are you sure that you are not putting the interests of your firm before those of the company and its shareholders? Is your marketing approach in consultancy compatible with professional independence?

5. Is your willingness to do the audit conditional on the client >

taking non-audit services from your firm? If so, how can you justify this derogation from ethical best practice?

6. Can you honestly say that you operate a zero tolerance policy for ethical breaches by everyone in the firm?

7. Are you sure that you would not regard staff as troublesome if they reported, in good faith, ethical lapses by people in the firm, especially if those lapses boosted the bottom line?

8. Is the incentive structure for partners and employees compatible with the public-interest function of auditing, or is the share of the spoils really based on an "eat what you kill" policy?

9. Would your decision to give the audit client a clean bill of health be the same if your firm had no non-audit fee income?

➤ CONCLUDING QUESTIONS FOR EMPLOYEES IN PROFESSIONAL FIRMS

1. As question 1 for partners.

2. As question 2 for partners.

3. As question 3 for partners.

4. If you observe that your superiors are not acting with due independence and objectivity in relation to questionable accounting treatments, are you prepared to make an issue of it?

● Case study:
VIVENDI & SALUSTRO-REYDEL

One of the biggest threats to the independence of the auditor occurs where the audit firm has, for want of a better phrase, a wonder client. A fast-growing client company that is hyperactive, making ever larger acquisitions and disposals, will have a growing need for both audit and non-audit services. It thus generates considerable revenue growth, not just for auditors but for all its financial service providers and professional advisers. Enron was a prime example, being a wonder client for the Houston practice of Andersen. Yet there have been countless others, more often than not involving a dominant, hard-driving CEO with a powerful aversion to applying a foot to the brake. Perhaps the most telling example is that of Vivendi Universal under the leadership of Jean-Marie Messier, who was unquestionably a wonder client for the French accountancy firm Salustro-Reydel.

Before the arrival of Messier as CEO in 1994, Générale des Eaux, as it was then known, was one of France's oldest companies, operating a water and sewerage business. Messier turned this pedestrian concern into a global media group through successive acquisitions in record time. He was the prototypical hard-driver. His finance director, Guillaume Hannezo, once wrote to him, "I've got the unpleasant feeling of being in a car whose driver is speeding up into the bends and that I'm in the death seat."[6] At the peak of Messier's acquisitive form Vivendi owned Universal Studios and Universal Music in the US, together with stakes in Cegetel, France's largest mobile phone group, Canal Plus, Europe's biggest pay TV company, and BSkyB, Rupert Murdoch's satellite TV company. Salustro-Reydel, which audited Vivendi jointly with Andersen, grew on the back of Vivendi's acquisition-powered growth. By 2001, according to *International Accounting Bulletin,* an industry newsletter, the firm derived 10 per cent of its €136 million ($207 million) revenues from Vivendi alone, making it very obviously vulnerable in the event of any disagreement with its powerful client.

CONVOLUTED ACCOUNTING

While Vivendi was busy with its acquisition spree the Commission des Opérations de Bourse (COB), the French securities watchdog, did not pay particularly close attention to the Vivendi accounts. But after the collapse of Enron it felt that it was on notice and applied closer scrutiny to the company's notoriously complicated financial statements. Its concerns immediately centred on the shareholding in BSkyB, where Vivendi's 22 per cent stake had been used as collateral for borrowings. Partly for tax reasons, transactions relating to the loan were structured in a very convoluted way, giving rise to difficult questions about how it should be accounted for in the 2001 results. Andersen proposed that the loan could be treated as a sale of the shares, which would have given rise to a profit of €1.5 billion ($1.9 billion) in the accounts, even though the profit had not been realised. Salustro-Reydel concurred with this treatment in its dialogue with the securities watchdog on the Vivendi numbers. Yet there were internal divisions on the point within the French audit firm. Xavier Paper, the man in charge of technical accounting matters at Salustro-Reydel, was convinced that this treatment was not correct under French accounting rules. He approached the COB directly to express his dissenting point of view, arguing that the accounting treatment gave a misleading picture of the substance of the transaction.

When the news of this move reached Vivendi, its deputy finance director, Dominique Gibert, fired off an email to Bernard Cattenoz, who bore responsibility at Salustro-Reydel for the Vivendi relationship: "I am furious to learn, on re-reading the COB's memo, that they have received advice from Xavier Paper… I therefore want you to send me a copy of Paper's memo and to let me know what action the practice intends to take to avoid repetition of this kind of problem, which could be highly prejudicial to VU." Two hours later Gibert's boss, Guillaume Hannezo, sent off another salvo by email: "There is a real problem in the way that Salustro functions and I hope that it will be dealt with one way or another as soon as possible." Later the same day Jean-Marie Messier added to the pressure with his own blast: "I am extremely shocked to learn all this. It raises a real ethical problem in terms of the professionalism of Salustro."

Jean-Claude Reydel, one of the audit firm's joint founders, and Bernard Cattenoz gave a grovelling response: "We wish to express our regret over the incidents provoked by one of our associates. On receipt of your letter we brought forward the board meeting to today, Sunday 3 March. During the meeting the board members unanimously decided to suspend Xavier Paper from his function as head of accounting methodology, with immediate effect." Unfortunately for Messier the COB intervened and Xavier Paper was reinstated. Worse was to come when these emails were extensively leaked to the press.

IMPROPER PRESSURE

On the company's side, it is clear that Messier equated ethical behaviour in auditing with blind loyalty to the management of a client company. The behaviour of the three Vivendi executives was a textbook example of bringing improper pressure to bear on an auditor. It was both unethical and obnoxious, since it amounted to bullying a small firm into removing or firing an individual who was bent on exercising an independent professional judgement based on a view that was subsequently endorsed as correct by the securities watchdog. Yet we would argue that in the circumstances the Vivendi executives probably deserved less in the way of censure than the auditors.

Accountancy is both an imprecise art and a matter of judgement. Vivendi at this point was in the midst of a serious cash crisis in which its credit lines with the banks were at risk of being withdrawn and the capital markets were becoming very twitchy. Against that background Messier and his colleagues were understandably worried that painting a less attractive picture in the accounts might damage the company. Most executives in that situation, where the survival of the company and their own jobs are in question, will do their best to maintain confidence even if the means employed are questionable. It is only human in a financial crisis to think that creative accounting is a lesser evil than the collapse of the company, even if the reality is that more damage may be done to creditors if creative accounting merely postpones the collapse.

On the auditors' side of the equation it has to be said that one of the purposes of the audit is precisely to protect shareholders, creditors and other stakeholders from the unethical behaviour of desperate people who are in a fix. Jean-Claude Reydel and Bernard Cattenoz were surely guilty of a serious ethical lapse. Their conception of the firm's business model, which was not shared by Xavier Paper, saw the client as Jean-Marie Messier, rather than the shareholders or other stakeholders in the company being audited. Yet all the senior people at Salustro-Reydel were surely at fault in permitting the firm to become so dependent on a single client. It was not merely that a reported 10 per cent of the revenue was coming from Vivendi. The firm was also involved in a joint venture with the company to develop accountancy software. Partners failed to ask themselves what threat to their professional independence was posed by this wonder client.

Standards in the French accountancy profession appear to have been deficient at this point in relation to the independence of the auditor, most notably on the score of the percentage of revenues derived by an audit firm from a single client. Legislation has since been introduced to fill the gap left open by the profession.

NOTES

1 *United States* v. *Arthur Young & Co.* (1984).

2 Depreciated: Did You Hear the One About the Accountant? It's Not Very Funny, *Wall Street Journal* (14 March 2002).

3 Auditors Need to Escape the Prisoner's Dilemma, *Financial Times* (16 May 2006).

4 *Auditor Independence, Conflict of Interest and Unconscious Intrusion of Bias*, by D. Moore, G. Lowenstein, L. Tanlu and M. Bazerman (2004).

5 We are indebted to James Montier of Dresdner Kleinwort Wasserstein for much of the discussion of auditors' psychology. See *Doing the Right Thing or The Psychology of Ethics*, DrKW Global Equity Strategy note (8 July 2005).

6 For an account of the rise and fall of Jean-Marie Messier at Vivendi Universal on which we have drawn for this case study, see *The Man Who Tried to Buy the World: Jean-Marie Messier and Vivendi Universal*, by Jo Johnson and Martine Orange (Viking 2003).

Chapter 12

ANALYSTS

SPEED-READ SUMMARY

- Once published, financial analysis quickly becomes a "public good" making it hard for researchers to charge users sufficiently to recover the costs of producing the research. As a result, research business models often contain a conflict of interest.

- This challenge is most visible in the investment banking world, but is not exclusive to it. Credit rating agencies, drug trials, management consultants, continuing education initiatives and universities also suffer from the difficulty of getting the users to pay for something that is likely to become a public good.

- Following the ethical abuses of the dotcom bubble (1999–2000), legal and regulatory changes have tried to reduce conflicts in investment banking research, primarily through greater disclosure and greater differentiation between financial promotion and independent analysis. However, these conflicts are not easily offset through disclosure alone.

- Analysts have a responsibility not just to disclose potential conflicts, but to avoid them and to avoid contrivances that are likely to bias their analysis.

- The modern temptation is for analysts to offload responsibility on to in-house compliance or ethics officers, or the accountants of the companies they are analysing or even the fund managers to whom they are "selling" their research. Caveat emptor has its limits.

In many countries across the world public confidence in the probity of financial institutions has eroded to the point where there is widespread cynicism about the workings of finance. This is unfortunate. For as we discussed in chapter 1 of this book, financial market participants need to have high ethical standards if the financial system is to do its job properly.

The practice of finance throws up many ethical challenges for participants. One of those challenges is that while the "sell-side" financial industry employs thousands of analysts who advise investors on the merits and risks of investments, investors do not pay for this research directly. There are many reasons why it is hard to charge for research, not least that if you are the first to charge and everyone else is still giving it away free, it is hard for you to survive long enough commercially for the industry's business model to change towards your own. Moreover, once research has entered the public domain, its price falls sharply towards the marginal cost of distributing the information. This problem is not unique to investment banking analysts. It is why the credit rating agencies also have an odd business model where ratings are paid for, not by the "users" of ratings, but by those being rated. This dichotomy between the cost of research – which for the major investment banks is in the hundreds of millions of US dollars – and the difficulty in charging directly for it – is a powerful source of potential conflict, bias and harm.

Traditionally, most researchers are employed by the sell-side of the financial industry, with the majority being employed by equity trading departments. The industry of financial analysis is experiencing some fluidity today, in part as a response by fund managers and separately by regulators, to the ethical abuses by the banks during the 1990s. Concern about residual conflicts of interest at banks has led institutional investors, insurance companies and even large pension plan sponsors to employ their own analysts. Independent research houses have sprung up. As the economics of selling analysis has become more marginal, some investment banks have been merging corporate bond and equity research departments.

Analysts do not sell themselves as financial promoters of a particular stock. They sell themselves as providing a balanced analysis of the merits and risks of investing or selling an instrument that they have previously announced that they "cover". They don't offer any guarantees, but in covering a stock or bond they purport to make best efforts in skill, prudence and diligence in making an investment judgement and to impart that information in a balanced way to a potential investor or seller. They owe their principal duty of care to these potential investors and sellers. However, since these investors do not pay directly for this analysis, the business model has evolved in perverse ways and is susceptible to conflict.

Charging for research because it will reveal knowledge a client didn't know they didn't know, but not giving the research before they have paid for it, is not an easy business model. Consequently banks provide free research hoping that it will spark discussions and conversations with clients that may lead clients to trade with the bank, whereupon the bank may make a trading commission or trading profit or advantage of some kind. The linkages between research and profits are present. But they can be tenuous and often hard to disentangle and measure: research may create a dialogue with clients and the dialogue may lead to a transaction and the transaction may be profitable. It must be remembered that clients trade with a bank for many reasons. A client could believe that a piece of research was so poor that she calls up the bank to complain and, while on the phone, decides to trade. Was that research "paid for" by the trade? Valuing research is highly uncertain.

As analysts know only too well, uncertainty reduces the valuation of people as well as businesses. Consequently, in the 1990s analysts quickly tuned in to more certain valuations of their work. They become linked with proprietary traders, corporate finance or investment banking departments. The links created turned potential conflict into an actual conflict of interest between the stated role of the analyst and what and how they were being rewarded – directly or indirectly.

ETHICAL ISSUES FOR ANALYSTS

The analyst's role at investment banks is largely reactive. It is interpreting and analysing the financial health of a company. The capacity for analysts to create contrivances and disguises is limited. Most ethical issues facing analysts are indeed conflicts of interest. These conflicts can create biased analysis. Finance professionals often retort that it is obvious that all research is biased and you just have to adjust for that bias. But that is easier said than done, especially for those with more limited access to information than financial professionals. Even if one attempts to adjust for this bias, it is necessary first to be aware of it. A recent survey of buy-side fund managers undertaken by MORI for the UK Financial Services Authority (FSA) revealed that 37 per cent of equity managers found it difficult to distinguish between objective and non-objective research emanating from sell-side analysts.[1] Moreover, being aware of a bias does not automatically mean you are able to adjust for it, especially if you rely on the same source for the information to make the adjustment. Retail investors in general who are less spoilt for choice on information and analysis find it harder still both to recognise and to adjust for perceived bias.

Conflicts of interests between clients of the brokerage function and the corporate finance function were extensively described and analysed after the 2000 stock market crash, as indeed they were after the 1929 crash. Generally banks earn direct fees from corporate finance work. For example they get fees by advising and arranging for a company to sell new stock through a rights issue or for trying to buy another company through a share swap. Obviously a bank is unlikely to win this mandate if its analyst is currently telling its investors to sell the stock. You can't blame the company for making that choice. However, a consequence of this is that in order to make sure they are in the frame for winning investment banking mandates, the bankers exert pressure on the analysts to avoid aggressively "selling" the stock.

Arguably the bankers too are just doing their job. They don't exert this pressure in a dictatorial way. Analysts are merely told that they can recommend "selling" the stock if they think that is the right recommendation, but given that the bank will lose several million dollars of fees, some of which would have found their way into the bonus pool that the analyst and her colleagues are paid from, the analyst just needs to be really, really sure that the sell recommendation is right. This leads to self-censorship. Given that all the available information should already be discounted in the price of a financial instrument, no one can be really, really sure about any price prediction in financial markets. Indeed, if there is anything they can be sure of, it is that in the past, being negative on stocks is often, though not always, unrewarded. The bank's conflict of interest – working for companies to sell stock to investors and working for investors to give them good investment advice – therefore leads inexorably to a bias in research. These biases do not generally cancel each other out which is why the bias lies in the same direction – "puffing" stocks higher.

Several studies show a relationship between investment banking priorities and investment research. According to a study by the UK Financial Services Authority in 2002, "buy" recommendations made by firms acting as corporate brokers or advisers to a company were nearly twice as high as where there was no relationship.[2] Sell recommendations are extremely rare, even during bear markets. To some extent this bias has been moderated by new regulations and settlements in the securities industry, but these are still only recent and there is evidence that bias still exists. This bias can easily lead to harm as investors end up being overly long those sectors about to have corporate finance activity. Academic research suggests that most corporate finance actions from rights issues, mergers and takeovers end up being value-destroying activities in practice.

CONFLICTS OF INTEREST IN HISTORY AND THE LAW

None of this is new. Similar conflicts of interest played a part in the 1929 stock market crash. The intertwining of commercial lending, stock trading and underwriting in the same institutions was so pervasive that the crash led to the closure of one in five banks in the USA. The 1933 Glass-Steagall Act tried to deal with these issues through federal insurance of small deposits and the separation of commercial banking from securities underwriting. Commercial banks were not allowed to issue, underwrite, sell or distribute any type of security with the exception of US government and government agency securities, and certain municipal bonds. However, regulations, consumerism and both national and international competitive pressures created an incentive for large diversified institutions to develop. Those that saw their future in that direction clamoured for a repeal of Glass-Steagall, and in 1999 they got their wish, as the Gramm-Leach-Bliley Act effectively removed laws separating commercial banking, investment banking and insurance activities.

The timing was at best unfortunate. Not long after the ink was dry on the new Act, we witnessed the unravelling of the most egregious examples of conflicts of interest leading to bias and potential harm: the dotcom bubble of 1998–2000. If the 1920s' boom and subsequent crash was about electricity, trains and cars, the 1990s boom was about mobile communications, "e-tailing", the internet, and supplier outsourcing. Many analysts and investment banks ended up embroiled in scandals that found their way to the courts. Record-breaking financial settlements were reached out of court – see the box on page 170.

That most of the settlements were out of court, with heavy fines but no apportioning of blame, is itself an important point. Public prosecutors took this path in part because while the ethical abuses appeared obvious, it would not have been easy to prove legal guilt based on information at that time. It had been one of the lessons of the 1930s that the complexity of the issues and ubiquity of practices made prosecutions difficult. In 1934, for example, after fighting for 18 months to extradite Mr Samuel Insull for bankruptcy, embezzlement and defrauding investors in what was the largest bankruptcy in American corporate history, Mr Insull was acquitted of all charges. That is not to say that the "perpetrators" got off lightly this time around or before. Prosecutors made the option of a court case or continued prosecution interest appear deeply unpleasant for institutions wanting to avoid further embarrassment. The settlements could have been worse, but they were substantial and onerous.

HENRY BLODGET & MERRILL LYNCH

The most famous example of analyst conflict of interest at the turn of the last century involved the internet "guru" Henry Blodget and his then employer Merrill Lynch. It was alleged that Mr Blodget and his team of analysts were unduly influenced by Merrill's investment banking division on decisions about providing research coverage for a particular stock and, more worryingly, on how to rate that stock. Far from there being a Chinese wall between investment banking and the analysts, it appeared that the analysts co-ordinated their research coverage in conjunction with the investment banking division in order to generate banking business. This collusion was further reinforced by analysts' compensation being linked to their contribution to bringing in investment banking business.

It is likely that Mr Blodget was little different from many analysts at the time – though by no means all – and indeed he may have been more self-conscious than some. His case attracted attention, however, because he was a well-known personality and Merrill Lynch was one of the largest brokers with a great many common investors. Henry Blodget became famous for tipping Amazon stock in 1998 to rise to $400 when it was just $243, whereupon it raced to $400 in under two months. Of course Mr Blodget like the authors of this book have made a number of wrong forecasts, but nobody does hype like Wall Street. What also made this case special was when New York Attorney General Eliot Spitzer released internal emails between Mr Blodget and his analysts. These showed that the analysts were far more negative in private than their public recommendations to investors and that they felt influenced by potential banking fees.

On 3 June 2000, Mr Blodget famously wrote "ATHM [excite@home] is such a piece of crap". But on the same day the broker published a note recommending investors "buy to strong buy".[3] On the day that Merrill Lynch initiated research coverage on GoTo.com with another strong buy recommendation, an institutional client emailed Mr Blodget to ask "what's so interesting about GoTo except banking fees???". He replied "nothin". This wasn't just repartee. It appeared that other analysts at Merrill had the same view. On 15 November 2000, Kirsten Campbell, a junior internet researcher at Merrill Lynch, emailed Mr Blodget regarding a research report on GoTo.com:

I don't want to be a whore for f-king mgmt. If 2-2 [Merrill Lynch's rating system which translated into "accumulate/buy"] means that we are putting half of Merrill retail into this stock because they are not accumulating it then I don't think that's the right thing to do. We are losing people and money and I don't like it. John and Mary Smith [fictional name for your average retail investor] are losing their retirement because we don't want Todd [GoTo.com's CFO] to be mad at us... the whole idea that we are independent of banking is a big lie.[4]

One of the most interesting points of the private email correspondence – and partly what made it a legal issue – was that the analysts appeared to be conscious of the conflicts of interest. They knew they were puffing stocks to help win banking mandates – they were even uneasy about it themselves. It is important to emphasise that those involved in ethical abuses are not devoid of conscience. Indeed, the premise of this book is that a pricking of that conscience with a few questions could save many from a lifetime of regrets. However weak, both conscience and honesty are visible in these emails. One could even feel sorry for the analysts and angrier with the bankers who exerted pressure, were it not for the fact that the analysts were simultaneously earning multi-million-pound bonuses.

■ The settlement between Wall Street firms and regulators

Under terms of the settlement, the ten Wall Street firms that were involved in the securities fraud agreed to pay $900 million to federal and state regulators, $85 million for investor education and $450 million to provide customers with independent research.

Citigroup's Smith Barney unit agreed to pay the largest single amount at $400 million. Merrill Lynch agreed to pay $100 million towards investor education and independent research and a $100 million penalty that the company had agreed to earlier. Regulators had charged three firms, Citigroup's Smith Barney, Merrill Lynch & Co and Credit Suisse First Boston, with committing fraud against investors but the fraud charges were dropped in the final settlement in exchange for the firms agreeing to reforms in the structure of their research operations.

The final settlement included guidelines on how and when a Wall Street investment banker will be able to interact with analysts. Firms were also to be given information on how to buy and distribute third-party research. Further, two independent monitors were to be assigned to each firm to oversee compliance with the settlement and the firm could only pick their own monitor if regulators approved the choice.[5]

MISSING ETHICAL QUESTIONS

What should the analysts of this world have asked themselves? In this book our chief ethical concerns relate to unresolved conflicts, contrivance, deceit and harm. But while this list triggers a number of examples, it is important to remember that we are looking upon these events in the cold light of day, from the vantage point of hindsight. At the time, pouring scorn on internet stocks appeared to be harming investors because they kept on going up, and to some extent, at the expense of alternative "old-economy" stocks. In 2000, Tony Dye, a value investor who had underweighted tech stocks in the belief that they would crash, was forced to leave Phillips & Drew Fund Management. This was as a result of the long period of equity underperformance his negative views on internet stocks had delivered until then. The popular idea that you needed a new form of valuation of these stocks may appear scandalous and hollow today, but for a significant period they appeared to many people to be right. Further, in some if not all of the research, the caveats and risks were highlighted by the analysts and ignored by the investors.

It remains, however, that the main cause of research bias was not ignorance but conflicts of interest. Analysts should have asked themselves whether they would have made the same recommendations or the same analysis if they were working for a firm without a corporate finance department or another compromising interest. They could have considered whether there were circumstances when they might have purchased these stocks for themselves. If the answers to these questions were yes – and in some cases they were – then the bias could be put down to a bout of collective optimism that often grips financial markets. It is not unethical to be wrong. But, if the answer was no, if when they said that the stock was really crap or a "piece of shit" they weren't just being cynical, but honestly felt that there were no circumstances in which they would consider buying the stock that day, then they acted unethically in advising investors to buy. They owed these investors a duty of care. They broadcasted their research as investment advice not as the financial promotion for banking business.

Related to these questions is the further question of unmitigated harm to others. Analysts should have asked themselves whether their actions were causing any unmitigated harm to others. Would

---

■ Jack Grubman

Jack Grubman, telecoms analyst for Salomon Smith Barney was accused in 2003 of upgrading his rating of AT&T in order to help his firm, Salomon, land part of a large stock deal AT&T was preparing in order to finance a spin-off of its wireless telephone unit.

The New York State Attorney General alleged that Mr Grubman also derived a personal benefit from the arrangement, as detailed in a two-page memo to his boss, Citigroup CEO Sandy Weill, entitled "AT&T and the 92nd Street Y". The impression the note gave was that if Weill, a member of AT&T's board and a close associate of AT&T CEO Michael Armstrong, would help Grubman's twins get into the 92nd Street Y, Grubman would become more "receptive" to AT&T's business model, which would help Salomon win the mandate. Not long after Mr Grubman sent his note, the philanthropic arm of Citigroup, the parent of Salomon Smith Barney, made a $1 million donation to the 92nd Street Y nursery school. It should be noted that this school was not a poor one serving a deprived neighbourhood but one of the mostly exclusive nurseries in Manhattan.

According to the eventual settlement, Mr Grubman does not accept these allegations, but has submitted to a lifetime ban on working in the securities industry in the future and a $15 million payment. In his memoirs, Mr Weill insists that he did not seek to exert improper influence on Mr Grubman. Yet for many, the story nicely captures the less-attractive human side of the dotcom saga. And when all is said and done, and whether you are earning $30 million or just $30,000, there was the perennial parenting problem of getting your kids into the right school.[6]

---

they have been happy for their nearest and dearest to be exposed to these recommendations? Would they want their mum and dad's retirement incomes to have been linked to their recommendations? From 1996 to 1999, as tech stocks outperformed other equity sectors, it is hard to say deliberate harm was being done to investors by recommending they own the sector. As the bubble burst and stocks remained on buy lists without any rationale other than the prospect of banking fees, then harm was being done, as brave Kirsten Campbell wrote in her email to Henry Blodget.

To avoid Mr Blodget's fate (an intelligent skilful analyst who knows more about stocks than many but is now barred from giving anyone investment advice) we recommend analysts ask themselves three broad questions whenever they get that sinking feeling in the pit of their stomach that there is an ethical dilemma.

It is important, of course, that employers help to create an environment in which employees are encouraged to ask these questions of themselves and the firm.

This may be a tough requirement, but it is interesting that of the banks and internet gurus that were the major players in the internet boom, a few were less tarred with indictments and heavy fines than others and these often worked for institutions with a less unbridled corporate culture or a culture that supported uncomfortable questions.

Asking questions could save a lot of money for everyone and could help to build a stronger financial edifice for us all.

➤ THE QUESTIONS

1. Do my investment recommendations owe anything to influences other than the best interests of investors? Are these influences disguised in some way? In other words would I follow my own recommendations were I in the same position as my investment clients?

2. Have I contrived an analysis that suits my personal interests to the potential disadvantage of investors? What would happen to the credibility of analysis in general if everyone followed my approach?

3. Could the articulation of my recommendations cause harm to others, in a way that could have been mitigated, such as by further analysis of risks and conditions? Would I want a broker giving advice to my mum and dad to follow my recommendations as they stand?

   And of course the answer to these questions above cannot be to the effect that I have devolved ethical responsibility to someone else such as the in-house compliance or ethics officers, or company accountants, or fund managers.

NOTES:

1   FSA, Ex-Post Analysis of FSA's Conduct of Business rules on Conflict of Interest in *Investment Research* (2005).

2   FSA, Discussion Paper 15, Investment Research – Conflicts & Other Issues (September 2005).

3   Taken from Litigation Release No. 18115 from United States District Court – Southern District of New York on 28 April 2003. For a full transcript, <www.sec.gov/litigation/complaints/comp18115b.htm>.

4   Taken from Litigation Release No. 18115 from United States District Court – Southern District of New York on 28 April 2003. For a full transcript, <www.sec.gov/litigation/complaints/comp18115b.htm>.

5   See "SEC, NY Attorney General, NASD, NASAA, NYSE and State Regulators Announce Historic Agreement to Reform Investment Practices" (Press Release, 20 December 2002).

6   Source for box: New York Attorney General's Office, *BusinessWeek*.

Chapter 13

REGULATORS

SPEED-READ SUMMARY

■ The world over, the form of public interest has moved from government ownership to regulation. Today, regulators play a large and perhaps growing role in the functioning of the modern economy. Few businesses do not interact with regulators and lawmakers on a regular basis.

■ Corruption of officials by companies seeking to influence them is primarily seen as something that happens to other people in other countries. The reality is that corruption of officials close to home is more widespread than acknowledged.

■ Governments try to limit corruption by banning gifts and limiting the ability of regulators to move into the private sector. These rules can be counter-productive.

■ Corruption is more subtle than officials accepting cash in a brown envelope or deposited in secret bank accounts. Today payments are made to "consultants" and "political advisers".

■ Where the monitoring and enforcement of anti-corruption rules are strong, the influence exerted on officials and regulators is subtle and sophisticated. One defence regulators should employ, is that before they consider any new regulation or regulatory decision, they should consider what that decision would look like if they were captured by those they are supposed to be regulating.

Over the past thirty years, the ownership of economic activity across the world has shifted substantially from the public sector to the private sector. This has been more dramatic in some countries, such as in the former Soviet Union, than in others, and the form of privatisation has differed across countries. In some cases, companies were privatised with no further government involvement in the sector other than the laws and regulations that broadly apply to all companies, such as those regarding product liability and health and safety. But in most cases, especially where the industry was inclined towards becoming a natural monopoly, such as the distribution of power and water, the public interest has shifted from ownership to regulation.

There are other industries which were not owned by the public sector, but were heavily controlled and regulated, such as broadcasting and banking. In parallel with the privatisation elsewhere, there has been in these areas liberalisation of regulatory regimes and a growing distance between regulator and government, often through the setting up of new regulatory agencies.

In the early days, this process was largely about getting "big government" out of the way of business. In recent years, government ownership has settled at a far more modest level and the momentum of liberalisation of regulations appears to be slowing down. Moreover, governments have become conscious of protecting public interests in new areas, for example with regard to the natural and built environment, genetic research and airwaves. Governments are taking to their new role as regulators with some zeal. The number of rules and regulators and the cost of regulatory agencies have all risen exponentially in industrial countries over the past ten years. Critics of this process argue that we are in danger of replacing the mixed economy with a regulated one. Less contentiously, regulators today play a large, perhaps increasing, role in business. From Microsoft defending itself against the charge of anti-competitive behaviour, or securities regulators asking Merrill Lynch to further separate its analysts and investment banking divisions, to your local restaurant seeking an extension of its licence to do business, few businesses do not interact on a regular basis with regulators or lawmakers in one form or another.

Ideally, regulation exists where there is a mismatch between private interests on one hand and public or social interests on the other, or where, for some reason, the market fails to function well. In the case of banking, for example, the social costs of a single bank going bust and triggering a panic that leads the banking system to shut down is far greater than the private costs for the owners of that bank. Consequently private owners of banks will underinvest in financial stability. Modern banking regulation is designed to get banks to internalise these "external" risks. In the case of retail distribution businesses like electricity distribution, there are enormous economies of scale and so the company with the lowest cost of capital is likely to end up owning the entire network, putting them in a position to extract monopoly profits from consumers. Electricity regulators try to limit abuse of consumers and, where possible, promote and reinforce competition. In the case of government procurement of large and unique defence systems that are of national security importance, the government cannot always use public tenders to get the best price or system, and government officials have to negotiate directly with defence companies to get the best deal for the exchequer.

CORRUPTION OF REGULATORS AND GOVERNMENT OFFICIALS

In each of the cases above, and others, regulators are dealing with and managing powerful commercial interests. Worldwide profits in the publicly quoted banking sector were approximately $100 billion in 2005. The defence and security industry is on par with the banking industry. There is substantial risk and concern that these commercial interests will curry favour with regulators. This concern is not without foundation. There have been many cases of companies employing unethical influence over governments in the procurement of defence contracts or the awarding of operational licences.

And these are not limited to problems of corrupt regulators and officials in developing countries, where accountability is often more difficult to enforce. There is unfortunately a long history of favouritism in the allocation of municipal contracts in the UK, US,

Japan and other developed economies. The corruption of regulators in developing countries remains a pressing problem, but of course the entities doing the corrupt payments are often companies based in rich countries that are supposed to comply with tough international anti-bribery rules. The enforcement of these regulations has been ineffective in many places.

According to a June 2006 report by Transparency International, fewer than 12 of the 30 members of the Organisation for Economic Co-operation and Development (a grouping of industrialised economies that has rules on international bribery of officials) have taken "significant action to enforce anti-bribery laws". It would appear that the OECD's zeal in attacking what it considers attractive money-laundering low-tax regimes in small developing countries appears to far outmatch its efforts to crack down on bribery of developing-country officials indulged in by companies in its own member countries. The Transparency International report particularly criticises Canada, Italy, Britain and Japan, countries that, with some irony, strongly condemned corruption in developing countries in the July 2006 G8 meeting.

Britain and the Netherlands have a notable absence of prosecutions, trials or convictions for the bribery of transnational company officials even though both countries have many large corporations involved in "risky sectors and markets" such as oil exploration and mining. According to the *Financial Times* (17 August 2006) "UK prosecutors complain that they are keen to pursue alleged bribery but the legal framework and political will to allow them to do so was lacking." Indeed allegations of corruption involving British companies often arise through investigations in countries that the British government would consider to have poor enforcement of global rules in other areas. In June 2006, an investigation by the World Bank on projects it helped to finance in Indonesia prompted an investigation by the Indonesian Anti-Corruption Commission into the alleged payment of $356,000 to Indonesian planning officials by WSP International, a division of the UK's WSP Group, which consults for large international development institutions.

One of the reasons that these regulatory abuses occur is that corruption is often considered something that "other" people do and in ways that we imagine other people indulge in: cash in brown envelopes being passed around or deposited in Swiss bank accounts. Closer to home, the same behaviour becomes sanitised as consulting services and commissions or lobbying. It was recently estimated that the cost of getting a large energy-related project completed in Nigeria, a country with a reputation for corruption, is 2 per cent of the total capital cost. Given that these projects are in the billions of dollars, this is a large sum that at the time scandalised those who were already susceptible to being scandalised. However, it is important to note that the costs of consultants and lobbyists to get a sensitive project approved in industrial countries is often in the region of 2 per cent.

In order to bring these issues closer to home to many readers, who might otherwise consider that corruption of officials is the preserve of some developing countries and therefore does not really affect them, we focus on two case studies in industrial countries. We also consider one area of potentially undue influence by companies on regulators, which is more about a shared culture and inherent regulatory weakness than it is about deposits in secret bank accounts. Both cases raise important ethical issues relevant to regulators and businesses.

● Case study:
MRS DARLEEN DRUYUN AND THE BOEING CORPORATION

This case study of the largest scandal at the Pentagon over the past twenty years, borrows from a series of investigations, most instigated by member of the US Senate Committee on Senate Armed Services, John McCain.

Most of its details have been taken from the CBS's *60 Minutes* and its reporter Scott Pelley's findings.[1]

● Case study: Mrs Darleen Druyun and the Boeing Corporation

From 1993 to 2003, Darleen Druyun was a senior Air Force official in charge of procurement, with an annual spend approaching $30 billion in the latter years. Even in terms of the US government, this is a large figure, larger than the cost of running many sizeable federal government departments like the Justice Department.

In 2000, Mrs Druyun was responsible for considering a $4 billion contract with Boeing to update the Air Force's C-130 planes. At the time Boeing was losing its competitive war in the commercial airline business with EADS, makers of Airbus. Darleen Druyun knew that she had Boeing's future in her hands. She contacted Michael Sears, the chief financial officer at Boeing, and asked him whether he had a job for her daughter's fiancé, Michael McKee. He was hired almost immediately. Three months later with the C-130 contract still being considered, she asked Mr Sears whether there was a job at Boeing for her daughter, Heather Druyun. Boeing responded positively. Under Pentagon rules, this was not illegal. But it was clearly an unethical conflict of interest which would cause the Air Force directly and taxpayers indirectly to suffer financial harm. Months after her daughter and son-in-law went to work at Boeing, Mrs Druyun awarded Boeing the $4 billion contract.

One of the factors in this episode was that a more transparent and public tender process in defence procurement could potentially undermine national security. However, the world over, national security exceptions are employed more often than they should be. They provide a convenient smokescreen behind which government officials can wield enormous personal power and behind which companies can try to influence officials.

In 2002, Boeing itself presented an audacious plan to the Pentagon to lease to the Air Force 100 767s as refuelling tankers at a staggering cost of $23.5 billion. To many experts this made little commercial sense. Moreover, given that the 767 was a version of a commercial airliner, it would appear that there was every opportunity for public tenders to bring the price down. Mrs Druyun's job was to get the Air Force the best price. But during the price negotiations, Boeing internal emails show that she was not using her best endeavour to get a better deal for the Air Force. After one meeting, a Boeing executive wrote: "Meeting today on price was very good. Darleen [Druyun] spent most of the time bringing the USAF price up to our number."

Senator John McCain who uncovered the emails in a Senate investigation into the costs of the refuelling tanker deal, said of Mrs Druyun's role, "Her job was to get the best possible price of the product for the American taxpayer. Instead, obviously she drove the price up to get the best possible

● Case study: Mrs Darleen Druyun and the Boeing Corporation

deal for Boeing Corporation." An audit by the Congressional Budget Office found Druyun's tanker deal would have overcharged taxpayers nearly $6 billion, approximately $50 per taxpayer, and more like 25 per cent on top of the real capital costs.

It would appear that Mrs Druyun's motives were not just to thank and support a company that had employed her daughter and son-in-law. In the midst of the tanker negotiations, Mrs Druyun's daughter, emailed Boeing CFO, Michael Sears, and revealed that her mother was retiring from the Air Force and was looking for a job. "She is very interested in talking to us, but we would have to give her something that would blow her out of the water." She also mentioned that Boeing had her mother's most admired quality: "honest values". (It is a disturbing, if perversely logical, trend that companies that loudly proclaim their honesty appear to attract the dishonest.) In November 2002, Druyun accepted an offer to be deputy general manager of Boeing's missile defence systems – with a $250,000 salary and a $50,000 signing bonus.

Assisting family members in getting a job does not violate Pentagon rules for ethical behaviour, but assisting yourself does – even if the original approach is made by someone else. It was this transgression of the rules that ultimately brought Mrs Druyun to book. In return for pleading guilty to violating conflict of interest rules, shouldering all the blame and admitting to supporting Boeing in other cases, Mrs Druyun was sentenced to 16 months in jail. Boeing's CEO, Phil Condit, and Mrs Druyun's boss at the Air Force, Marvin Sambur, also resigned.

Our concerns are less with Mrs Druyun's and Boeing's precise transgression of the law. Long before she and Boeing did anything illegal they did things that were unethical. She made decisions that harmed the government financially, in part because her family's employment at Boeing influenced her decisions. Two other interesting points come to mind. First, in the words of Senator John McCain, "Where was the United States Air Force? Where was the Department of Defense in this? How could she do all this alone?" How could Marvin Sambur not know what Mrs Druyun was doing? An ethical concern here is that a large number of people in Boeing and the Air Force turned a blind eye to the appearance and reality of favouritism in multi-billion-dollar contracts.

A further important issue is to what extent did Mrs Druyun allow Boeing to inflate the contract price, not in the clear expectation of participating in the end-of-year bonus pool, as in the case of analyst conflicts of interest, but in the expectation that one day in the future, Boeing may be of assistance to her? This kind of influence of officials or of companies through not-yet-fulfilled expectations is far harder to identify and control. In the next case study we look at even more subtle forms of influence than the eventual prospect of a $250,000 job offer.

BIG BANKS AND THE NEW BASEL CAPITAL ACCORD

The authors believe that the new Capital Accord for large and internationally important financial institutions written by the Basel Committee of developed country central bankers and regulators who meet in the Swiss town of Basel (Basel II) has the hallmarks of regulatory capture by the large banks they are supposed to be regulating.[2] The capture has been so sophisticated and subtle, without any hint of illegality, that many of those that have been captured by the large banks may not realise it themselves.

Few would argue against the observation that the new accord favours large banks in industrial economies. Under the new rules, banks with complex credit default models and large datasets more affordable for large banks in industrial countries, are rewarded with lower capital charges from their regulators, with little emphasis on their history of credit management. Capital charges are rather like taxes. The question is whether this tax-cut concession for largeness is merely a side effect of supporting good behaviour, or a result of capture of the regulators by large banks. This is hard to establish definitively, but the evidence points in the direction of capture. The objectives of both regulation and good banking would not lead to such a focus on prescriptive and complex models and datasets that inevitably favours large banks.

There are two primary purposes of bank regulation: one is consumer protection and the second is the avoidance of systemic risks. Large banks are far more systemic-related than small institutions (that is, as long as consumer-protection regulation does not encourage all small institutions to behave as if they are one large bank, as was arguably the case with the Savings and Loans institutions in the United States in the 1980s and with hire–purchase institutions in the UK in the 1970s). In theory, the more systemic the institution the greater should be its capital charges, so that only the most efficient and well-managed institutions will grow larger while the less efficient will remain mid-sized. This would encourage a competitive banking market of institutions that innovate to the benefit of consumers, but with less risk to the financial system. Instead, regulation has created advantages to size that have encouraged the development of a few large banks, too large to innovate, but also too large to fail lest they trigger a systemic crisis. This is most stark in the UK.

Large banks can more easily show their supervisors that they have large and complex computer models for monitoring credit – so large and complex that many supervisors do not understand them. These computer models are sometimes poor at estimating credit risks, perhaps because in the effort to make them universal they use too many assumptions. This focus in Basel II on "process" (how big your model is) rather than "results" (how good your model is at predicting credit risks), favours larger banks and does not reward relationships or specialised knowledge that can be important for risk management as well as for consumers. Not surprisingly, it does not necessarily deliver better credit results (though we need to see the results across a full economic cycle before we can judge that correctly). The point is that lower capital charges for systemically important institutions should come as a result of proven results, not the size of their in-house computer. If this were the case, smaller institutions that invest in knowing their customers well, would be able to compete, adding a diversity that would strengthen the financial system.

The large banks appear to have "sold" regulators the pre-eminence of "risk sensitivity" which is the philosophy underpinning Basel II. This sounds so right that it has escaped sufficient scrutiny. But once consumers are protected through product-liability legislation, compensation schemes and tough jail sentences for breaches of rules to protect "small" consumers from fraud, the only risk that regulators should be concerned with is the risk to the financial system, not the level of risk for an individual bank. The two are not necessarily the same. Risk sensitivity is a meaningless statement without identifying what risks you are being sensitive to. A bank can run large private risks for the bank with minimal systemic risk, or, for example, a bank involved in the payments or settlements systems can run small risks for the bank but large systemic risks. Rather than focusing on identifying, measuring and minimising systemic risks – the purpose of regulation – regulators, in the name of risk sensitivity, are fretting about how to align regulatory capital with the bank's private risks – which banks should be sufficiently incentivised to do in the first place.

It is possible that the Basel Committee was not captured by the large banks in developing the new rules. If you were to dream up a regulatory system where the points of regulation connect with the points of market failure and no more, it would look very different to Basel II. To deal with systemic risks, such a system would focus on counter-cyclical charges, because the course of the economic cycle is a major source of systemic risk with an additional charge for institutions considered systemic as a result of their business and reach. Basel II has the opposite effect, being pro-cyclical and awarding large systemically important institutions discounts on their capital charges. To protect consumers you might have a private deposit insurance scheme where safe, small institutions had lower insurance premiums than large, risky ones. Basel II has the opposite effect, with small institutions facing larger regulatory costs as a per cent of total costs than large institutions, and large institutions benefiting from an effective government guarantee. But if the Basel Committee was captured, how was it done? Although banking regulation appears to be an arcane subject, the methods of capture by the banks over the regulators have much to instruct us in other areas.

REGULATORY CAPTURE
In the case of Basel, there were two avenues of capture. First, banks captured the regulators through complexity. In industrial countries, complexity is often the main avenue of regulatory capture. By paying for the best consultants to highlight every exception to every rule, the resulting body of rules became so unwieldy and complex that bankers rather than regulators are best paid for the trouble to understand them. The first Basel Accord was essentially eight pages long. The second was 600 pages in draft, and, after criticism from your authors and others, has been pinned

back to around 300 pages. In most places around the world, regulatory capacity is limited and in managing a complex rule book the large banks have the advantage over the regulators. Indeed, this is one of the reasons why outside the EU so many regulators are reluctant to adopt the new rules.

The other form of capture relates to the case of Darleen Druyun and Boeing. Today, CEOs and chairmen play musical chairs at the very top of public and private financial institutions and regulatory bodies – which is an indication of the importance the private sector now pays to regulation. This is most visible in countries where finance ministers do not need to hold elected office, such as the United States, where senior bankers have become treasury secretary and then gone back. The most likely next job for a deputy governor of a central bank with more than one deputy is the chairmanship of a bank rather than the governorship. None of this is unique to finance. Former NASA astronauts can be found on the boards of companies that want to sell products to NASA.

This relationship can have many benefits for all parties, especially with regards to a knowledge transfer. But the relationship is probably in the public sector's favour when a senior figure moves from the private sector to be regulator, rather than the other way around. Given this game of musical chairs, it does not pay for a senior figure to be too adversarial during his or her time at the head of a regulatory body. Especially when tenure in senior public jobs can be short, poorly paid comparatively and open to so much political pressure; a parachute into a private sector job is an important personal career safety device. In some countries, senior public jobs are seen as the burden one must bear for a short time, in order to get to the more comfortable senior private jobs. But the point is that this is an environment for officials and regulators to share a similar and supportive culture where influence is as much through shared ideas and country clubs rather than monetary incentives. At the very least, it is an environment where officials have their guard down against potential capture.

CONCLUSION, REMEDIES AND QUESTIONS
Well-judged, monitored and enforced controls are a key line of

defence against ethical abuse of the national purse or public interest by companies wielding undue influence over regulators. Most regulatory bodies have very tight controls on the acceptance of gifts or negotiating future positions of employment with those the regulator should be regulating. In the United States, the most many government regulators are allowed to accept, as a gift from those they regulate, is a cup of coffee. These rules are designed to eliminate harmful bias caused by conflicts of interest. However, we wonder whether they can be counter-productive. Creating bars between the private and public sectors and, in place of perks, making them wear hair shirts to show off their integrity, allows the public sector to pay and treat regulators substantially worse than they would be treated in the private sector, making regulators vulnerable to capture by the private sector.

One way around this would be to seek a two-way flow between the public and private sectors, by recruiting a number of senior managers from the private sector to work for the regulator. This would not only improve the regulators' diversity of knowledge and experiences, but would require regulators to provide a more competitive pay structure. This was an approach pursued by Sir Howard Davies during his chairmanship of the UK Financial Services Authority. It was also pursued by the US Securities and Exchange Commission since its inception in the 1930s.

The first line of defence against ethical abuse is, of course, the integrity of regulators. It is possible that those who select a job in regulation in the first place, despite the more attractive pay and perks available elsewhere, may start off with a more developed sense of personal integrity than is the norm. However, as we have discussed throughout this book, in the heat of the moment many people do things that they would regret with greater reflection. We feel that the regret can be avoided if regulators and others continuously ask themselves a few simple questions.

➤ QUESTIONS TO BE ASKED

1. **Am I devolving ethical responsibility to someone else – an in-house lawyer, an ethics officer, or even not someone, but something like the conveniently superficial reading of an ethics code?**

We argue in chapters 1 and 2, that individual responsibility cannot be hung up with the coats when entering the office every day, but has to be worn continuously.

2. **Do I have a disguised conflict between the public interest I am employed to defend and an alternative private interest?**

Mrs Druyun had a conflict between beating down Boeing's initial prices and pleasing Boeing sufficiently that they would be happy to reward members of her family and one day herself with well-paid employment.

3. **Is unmitigated harm being caused by my actions?**

Mrs Druyun and Boeing together caused immense harm to the public purse. In the pursuit of safe banks, bank regulators may have shifted financial risk to pensioners. Pension funds are regulated by others, but bank regulators have an ethical duty to consider such a possibility and to consider ways of mitigating the harm.

4. **Have I contrived a situation that puts myself, my future potential employers or partners at an advantage to others?**

Arguably, the Basel Committee of bank regulators has developed a rule book that puts big banks at an advantage to small banks in a way that is not necessary for good regulation or good banking. It is equally likely that this was not as a result of any immediate or calculated pecuniary gain, but through a "culture" that lowers the regulators' guard ➤

against developments that are made in the name of good regulation, but have the effect of supporting large banks.

Regulators may raise their guard by asking themselves a related question before they consider any new regulation: what would this regulation look like if I were captured by the most powerful of the interests that I am here to regulate? Ideally, the answer to this question should be written down, sent to members of the press, framed and hung up where it can be seen and remembered on a daily basis.

● Case study on self-regulation:
LLOYD'S AND THE CITY

Markets have often worked well on the basis of self-regulation. And for many years the City of London, the hub of the British financial system, was regarded as a classic example of effective self-regulation, based largely on an internal set of rules, or by-laws, not unlike those of a London gentleman's club. The strength of such a system lies in the trust that exists between market practitioners who know each other and share a common set of values reflected in the club rules. This obviates the need for heavy-handed bureaucracy, while peer pressure ensures that members observe the commands of the rule book. Those who misbehave are quickly ejected. The snag with this approach to governance is that clubs all too easily become inward-looking and out of touch with the standards prevailing outside. When that happens, the members start to put their own interests before those of the clients they are supposed to serve. If the club is opened to outsiders the sense of solidarity that stems from a perception of common interest may be undermined. Nothing illustrates these points better than the affairs of the Lloyd's of London insurance market in the late 20th century.

Lloyd's had its origins in a 17th-century coffee house that played host to the City's insurance underwriters. The market retained some of that sense of informality even in the period that followed the Second World War. Underwriting members of the club, known as "names", provided insurance cover for policyholders seeking cover against big risks ranging from marine underwriting for ships to insurance for oil rigs. While there were working members of the club, the great majority of names were external members, prepared to take on unlimited liability in exchange for the insurance profits and the special opportunities for tax avoidance that Lloyd's privileged status presented. They were an exclusive group because members had to show they had substantial capital before being allowed to underwrite the big risks taken on at Lloyd's. And they were yet more exclusive because foreigners were excluded from membership before 1969 and women before 1970.

Lloyd's governing body, the Committee, derived its ability to enforce its rules and expel miscreants through private Acts of Parliament starting with the legislation that gave the society incorporated status in 1871. But before the Lloyd's Act of 1982 the legislative framework was of the minimalist variety and the by-laws' strictures on conflicts of interest were weak. Because of the difficulty of obtaining agreement at general meetings to toughen the by-laws, discipline was imposed largely through undertakings given by working members when they joined the market or were granted permission to do particular business in the market.

ENTREPRENEURIAL CULTURE

The club ethos fostered a much more entrepreneurial culture than in large insurance companies. Lloyd's in the heyday of self-regulation was highly innovative. It insured anything from the legs of Hollywood star Betty Grable to moon shots. Lloyd's underwriting syndicates were also capable of losing hundreds of millions on amateurish bets such as guaranteeing the residual value of mainframe computers when leases came to an end. This was, in effect, a bet against IBM's ability to make its own product line obsolete. It also contravened one of Lloyd's own long-standing rules: not to give financial guarantees. With the benefit of hindsight, this was one of several early indications of a flawed culture at this hallowed institution. Evidence of unethical behaviour finally surfaced in a big way after a US insurance broker, Alexander & Alexander, took over Alexander Howden Group, a large broker and underwriting manager which was deeply involved in insurance and reinsurance at Lloyd's. A routine audit after the takeover threw up evidence that funds had been diverted into Howden directors' pockets. Financial scandals then erupted at PCW Underwriting Agencies and at syndicates that had been doing business with a Bermudan company called Fidentia Marine Insurance.

The investigations that followed showed that funds had been misappropriated by working members of Lloyd's on an impressive scale.

Secret profits had been made at external members' expense where working members had channelled reinsurance business to offshore companies where they, their friends and associates were shareholders. Directors of Lloyd's agencies had steered more profitable business to so-called "baby syndicates" which were run for their benefit. This proved to be one of several examples of funds being manipulated between syndicates at the expense of external members.

AN OUTRIGHT SCAM

This behaviour was clearly unethical. Working members of the club were rigging the market in their own interests. The scam was particularly egregious because the outside names who were being saddled with all the worst risks had unlimited liability. While, in the event, Lloyd's was not notably fierce in its handling of names that were unable to pay up, many of the victims of the scams were condemned to live their lives in straitened circumstances. So why did self-regulation fail so spectacularly at this venerable financial market? Why were the ethical lapses so outrageous?

One reason was that the sense of solidarity was seriously eroded because of the post-war growth of the insurance market. Insurance is a capital intensive business and the risks have grown considerably in size over the past half century or so. As a result Lloyd's was forced to go outside its narrow, well-heeled membership to secure capital to finance its growth and maintain a decent share of the global insurance market. In the 1970s it had just 6,001 members, of whom 4,919 were external. By 1986, when a committee under Sir Patrick Neill reported on regulatory failures at Lloyd's, the membership was 28,944, of whom 23,547 were external. As the Neill Committee remarked, the defects of the self-regulatory system, in dealing with conflicts of interest, could be tolerated while the size of the society was relatively small. But in a body that had become less club-like, conflicts of interest were more likely to be abused.

Yet the most extraordinary aspect of the problems at Lloyd's was that so many people in the market were unaware that much of what had happened was not just unethical but illegal. As the Neill Committee report put it:

Apart from these particular matters… the investigations drew attention to an absence of understanding on the part of many working members of the principles of the law of agency. The Lloyd's investigators into PCW told the Corporation (in a letter dated 20 January 1984) that it was apparent to them that many members of the Lloyd's community in senior positions 'were not even vaguely aware' of the legal obligations on agents to act at all times in the best interests of their principals, not to make secret profits at their principals' expense and to disclose fully all matters affecting their relationship with their principals.

In short, Lloyd's offers a perfect illustration of how the self-regulatory club ethic can lag ethical trends in wider society. The Committee and working members of Lloyd's were living in an ethical time warp. They were not asking even the most basic question that should always be raised in a principal–agent relationship: am I putting my own interests before those of the clients being served?

THE STOCK EXCHANGE CLUB

The experience at Lloyd's of London was echoed at much the same time but in a less egregious way by changes at the London stock exchange. In the early 1980s the exchange still had many characteristics of a London club, despite its importance for the functioning of the wider economy. And under legislation introduced by a Labour government in the 1970s there was a risk that its dealing system might have been regarded as a restrictive practice. Under this system market makers, known as jobbers, were not allowed to deal directly with the investing public, but were obliged to go through brokers on the exchange. For their part, brokers acting for investment clients were not allowed to act as principal, holding shares for their own account. This was known as a "single capacity" system, because members of the exchange could only act in the capacity either of a market maker or a broker, but not both. An important advantage of the system was that it reduced the scope for conflicts of interest. Brokers' clients knew that the brokers did not have a position in the shares in which they were carrying out transactions, so advice and dealing behaviour were not distorted by the imperatives of a broker's own dealing book.

As part of a compromise between the stock exchange and the competition authorities in the early 1980s, the exchange agreed to shift to an American-style dual capacity system in which the barriers between jobbing and broking were removed. Foreigners, hitherto excluded from the exchange, were allowed in. In the so-called Big Bang that followed, there was a large inflow of foreign capital and a wave of takeovers and mergers in both broking and jobbing. The aim was to create financial conglomerates capable of making markets, broking and carrying out research, while simultaneously conducting investment banking activities such as capital raising and providing advice on mergers and acquisitions. Many British firms were taken over. As so often in periods of dramatic corporate change, managements did not always send clear signals to employees in the newly merged firms as to the values of the enlarged organisations. And as usually happens in any move to deregulate markets, profits were eventually squeezed. There was then a temptation for people to cut corners in a system where the scope for conflicts of interest had greatly increased and the solidarity that had accompanied the old club ethos had gone.

REGULATORY EXCESS

While the abuses were minor when compared with the criminality at Lloyd's, they were sufficient to prompt the new post-Big Bang securities watchdog, the Securities and Investments Board, to put out an elaborate and excessively detailed set of rules. This is a pattern repeated throughout the world's financial markets: Where there are ethical lapses, excessively bureaucratic legislation or regulation usually follows in an attempt to restore confidence in the marketplace. To change the metaphor, the regulatory tide is then exceptionally difficult to roll back. The regulatory ratchet is not uniformly rigid. In London the Financial Services Authority that now supervises all the markets operates a principles-based regime rather than a legalistic rule book of the kind administered by its predecessor body. That said, it continues to be criticised by practitioners for a heavy-handed approach.

Is a reversion to more self-regulation a remotely realistic possibility? No doubt there is still some role for self-regulation in parts of the business and financial system. But the lessons of history suggest that as a means of regulating the overall framework, self-regulation is unlikely to stage a big comeback. It took the best part of 70 years for the United States to rid itself of the restrictive financial and securities legislation introduced by the Glass-Steagall Act after the 1929 crash. No sooner had the legislation been repealed than the Enron crisis led to the Sarbanes-Oxley Act and the campaign by Eliot Spitzer, the New York state attorney general, to impose new restrictions on investment banks. The chief role for self-regulation will therefore tend to be in newer markets where the heavy-handed machinery of regulation has lagged behind economic developments. Even so, the cycle of market euphoria, scandals and collapses, followed by regulatory tightening, seems, over the past century, to have become endemic.

NOTES:

1   60 Minutes II, 4 January 2005, <www.cbsnews.com/stories/2005/01/04/60II/main664652.shtml>.

2   See Basle II, <www.bis.org/publ/bcbsca.htm> and Avinash D. Persaud, "The New Capital Accord from Basel, Inaugural Lecture, Gresham College, October 2001.

PART 4: Conclusion

Chapter 14

FINALE

Transactions invariably took place at the edge of feasibility, conducted against a competitive background under great time pressure. I found few committees of experts considering all the available evidence in wise conclave. Much more typical were decisions taken on the fly, by whoever happened to be available, based on a fraction of the full information.[1]

David Freud

This description of the way a large part of finance works, chimes with the authors' own observations. Quite apart from what this says about the efficiency of shareholder capitalism, this view of the way finance works "on the ground" underscores the premise of this book. Many financial participants get swept along into actions from which on greater reflection they might well recoil. In finance, disproportionately large financial incentives are based around closing the deal, trade, or merger or acquisition. This leads to a laser-beam focus on the narrow issues related to getting the deal done. What other industries would today consider to be issues of "sustainability", whether they relate to financial matters or trust-based relationships, seldom get anything more than a perfunctory nod. The ethical abuses that arise as a result of this process have significant consequences for individuals, companies, the finance industry and the wider public.

As we discussed in chapter 1, trust is fundamental to business relations and to the efficient working of markets. Trust has social value. It also has implications for cost and efficiency. But that does not mean it is optimally imposed on professionals through legislation or regulation. An over reliance on laws and regulations has costs. The more transactions have to be governed or regulated by contract, the more cumbersome and costly business becomes, because everything has to be negotiated, agreed, monitored and sometimes litigated and enforced. Moreover, many entrepreneurial initiatives are founded upon relationships that, initially, are too undefined to be contractually drawn up. If trust does not exist outside legal contract, many of these relationships would flounder before business developed. Entrepreneurship would be cut short. Indeed, there is a relationship between financial development and the levels of trust in an economy.

Put crudely, to business and finance professionals, personal and corporate ethics are in many cases an efficient substitute for external regulation and internal control within the company. Ethical values are also the glue that holds large organisations together. The collapse of Enron, WorldCom, Andersen and sundry others demonstrates what can happen when ethics go out of the window. At a conceptual level, this makes sense and is readily agreed upon. But making this work at a practical level remains a challenge.

A MORI poll in the UK in 2004, just two to three years after the sordid details of many dotcom "bezzles" had come to light, showed that when prompted, only 42 per cent of institutional investors said they took into account honesty and integrity in making judgements about investing in companies. When not prompted, this figure fell to 6 per cent. It seems the notion, so clearly demonstrated in the aftermath of the dotcom bubble, that the character and values of a company matter, has only marginally penetrated the investment process. This does not encourage company management to take ethics seriously. And if investors and managers do not take ethics seriously, employees and professional service providers will not find it conducive and may find it career-threatening to do so. (We looked at whistleblowing in an earlier chapter and we will touch on the role of leadership below.) The purpose of this book is to encourage greater ethical reflection by business and financial professionals: partly by emphasising that ethics requires personal responsibility and is not to be "outsourced" to ethics and compliance officers, or auditors and lawyers; and partly by helping to raise some key questions that market participants could ask themselves. We shall return to these questions and their genesis at the end of this chapter.

It is worth asking whether we need any more elaboration than simply requiring finance and business professionals to only do those things they would be content to be on the receiving end of themselves. This is a principle that can be found in many philosophies and religions from Christianity to Hinduism as well as in humanism. However, the authors' observation is that this principle would not, on its own, work well in finance. Many finance professionals consider that they live in a part of the jungle where the survival of the fittest is the only rule that applies and almost any thing is "fair game". Many finance professionals expect their counterparties to have conflicts of interest, to be involved in contrivances to obtain bargains and not to care too much about it. The immediate reaction of many traders to the Citigroup bond trade was jealous admiration. Doing to your neighbour what you would have him do to you, does not provide much restraint in the practice of finance.

MUCH HAS CHANGED AND LITTLE HAS CHANGED

In chapter 10 on bankers we described the way legislation tends to play catch-up with ethical abuses. After each crisis, legislators rush to draft new legislation to ensure the abuses could not happen again. Part of their motivation is to deflect popular anger at the abuses from themselves by showing that they are taking them very seriously. This process leads to rushed legislation in the heat of the moment that is often disproportionate and ill judged. Today's legislative and regulatory environment in finance and business relates largely to the "bezzle" of the dotcom era and of the occasions of "crony-capitalism" during the mid-1990s in the newly industrialising Asian economies.

The primary legislative response to the dotcom "bezzle" was the Sarbanes-Oxley Act in the US that was rushed through Congress in 2002. SOX as it is widely known is having a pervasive impact on corporate behaviour, and because it covers companies with listings on US exchanges, the impact goes far beyond US territory. Today, it is deterring US listing. Spurred on, in part by SOX, corporate governance and ethics codes have proliferated across the world – every self-respecting company has one. And to support the burgeoning industry of ethics officers and ethical mission writing, the study of business ethics rolls unstoppably on. Every self-respecting university has a course or two on business ethics.

A measure of the changed environment is the advent of TV ads that are not actually trying to sell anything other than the good ethics of companies. In the past, adverts for oil companies would be about the potency of the oil they sell, which was often conveyed with roaring tigers, fast cars and much machismo. Today, the ads are more likely to boast environmental scientists wearing yellow anoraks testing soil samples or tropical fish blissfully swimming past an underwater pipeline. Yet despite this refreshing concern for doing business in an ethical manner, the corporate scandals just keep coming.

Whistleblowers appear to have missed dubious behaviour related to government contracts at Haliburton, though not, eventually, at Boeing. Senior managers appear to have been unaware of the ethically dubious intentions of the Citigroup government bond traders. The boards and their auditors appear to have been remiss at Parmalat and Volkswagen. Bankers may have failed to uncover inappropriate dealings at Refco and AIG. The list goes on. And across a wide range of companies, boardroom pay continues its exponential rise often unrelated to corporate performance. This is well illustrated by the practice of managers asking compliant boards to reset stock options that otherwise would be worthless.

WHY HAVE THE CODES NOT WORKED?

We fear that the extraordinary expansion of legislation and governance codes since Enron has exacerbated the problem by encouraging a compliance culture rather than an ethics culture. Too many boards have outsourced the task of ethics to ethics officers, who in turn have relied on consultants to define the company's values. Ethics have become something that "other people" in the organisation worry about, leaving everyone else unfettered by ethical concerns. Ethics and governance are reduced to a box-ticking exercise, while many ethical codes are cynical public relations exercises that have little to do with critically examining behaviour. Of course, this cynical attitude is not universal as we touched on in chapter 5 on investing and speculating. We believe that an ethics culture must start, not with a code, but with individual responsibility. This would not mean a dysfunctional organisation, where individual employees pick and choose what they wish to do on the basis of their personal ethics. It should mean an organisation open to questioning and amending its behaviour, in response to the ethical considerations of its employees, managers and shareholders, and, in appropriate measure, its clients, business partners and community.

Besides the notion that ethics are "other people's" problems, the other main obstacle to an effective ethical culture is short-term incentive structures. Post-SOX, most recent ethical abuses have been about creative accounting to keep up the value of remuneration packages for senior managers. This has taken many forms, from boosting revenues in spurious ways, to the ethically dubious practice of backdating and springloading stock options. They have occurred in an environment where much boardroom pay continues to take the form of equity and stock options or at least "performance-related" pay when the only performance in question is the short-term performance of the share price. Add in the fact that chief executive officers are under greater pressure than ever before from fund managers and analysts to "hit the numbers" and you have the nub of the problem. Short-term incentive structures in the boardroom and below are pushing in a direction that is at odds with ethical behaviour and, often, commercially unsupportable.

Although this poor alignment between remuneration packages and the sustainability and ethics of a company's performance lies at the centre of many ethical abuses, it is not addressed by the Sarbanes-Oxley Act. Its requirement for companies to have a code of ethics for the CEO and the chief financial officer implicitly assumes that you can legislate people into good behaviour. But even for those companies that do take ethics seriously, the rate of corporate change, with frequent takeovers, divestments and redundancies, makes it harder to hold on to core values.

The law alone is not enough to ensure that corporate behaviour is aligned with the wider interests of society and industry. It invariably codifies the lowest common denominator, while lagging behind changes in the way the economy and markets evolve. In countries where enforcement is weak, companies can pursue unethical courses of action very profitably for a while, but at a high cost to local populations. And corporate activity has side effects – externalities – that are not adequately regulated by the market or by laws and regulations. So there is a need for ethical behaviour, especially in the grey areas where managers face conflicting priorities. It follows that restoring trust and establishing a more ethical corporate culture are worthwhile objectives. That means addressing flawed incentives and the "hitting the numbers" culture.

LEADERSHIP

The misalignment between remuneration and corporate sustainability and ethics is something which relates largely to managers and leaders. But the behaviour of leaders affects the entire organisation. In this book we place great emphasis on individual responsibility. We object to professionals, be they treasurers, analysts, bankers, risk managers, auditors or others, devolving their ethical responsibility to their managers or advisers. But business leaders have additional responsibilities for creating the kind of environment in which ethical behaviour can exist. An ethical culture has to be embedded, which takes time, training and effort. People at the top have to show, in part by example, that they do not expect employees to shed their moral values (integrity) when they walk through the company door.

That means listening to concerns of employees, whether directly or through speak-up or helplines. It means conveying the message that beating targets and winning business at any cost fly in the face of what the company is about. It means designing reward systems that reflect the requirement for ethical behaviour and adherence to codes. Above all, management should avoid the crass error perpetrated at Enron whereby people who violated the company's stated values were treated as heroes, if the violation was potentially helpful to the bottom line.

In writing codes of ethics, it is also vital for managers to engage employees throughout the company. A code handed down from on high, without consultation, will be treated with the scepticism it deserves. A code that is substantially the work of outside consultants is unlikely to be very effective because it will not embody the best of the internal standards, traditions and values of the company. Internal development or input is helpful to the embedding process. Leadership also means setting an example that you would want others to follow. This is more about openness, responsiveness and courage than being a saint or being always beyond reproach. And it is particularly about taking ownership of decisions and actions. There are many things that managers should delegate to others but ethical responsibility is not one of them.

THE GENESIS OF OUR QUESTIONS

John Maynard Keynes famously said that "practical men, who believe themselves to be quite exempt from any intellectual influence, are usually the slaves of some defunct economist". We are conscious that while this book has been written from a practical point of view without reference to the substantial body of work on moral philosophy and ethics, that our perspective inevitably borrows from certain philosophical traditions. Young recruits to the finance industry, overawed by its abundant use of modern technology, may wrongly consider finance a modern endeavour that breaks new ground and requires a new ethic, but the issues of ethical practice that we have discussed in this book are as old as the hills. They are well illustrated in the debate between Arjuna and Krishna in the 6th-century BC story of the *Mahabharata*, where Krishna emphasises doing one's duty, while Arjuna focuses on avoiding bad consequences. We do not take sides in this well-reasoned tussle, but consider both duty and consequences in arriving at some questions finance professionals should ask themselves to help them consider the integrity of their actions. Adam Smith argued that our "first perceptions" of right and wrong "cannot be the object of reason, but of immediate sense and feeling".[2] For those, perhaps like David Hume, who believe that there can be no such thing as practical reason, our questions are there to help individuals sort out their feelings and senses. For others, they are there to help reason.[3]

Having said that we do not take sides in the Arjuna–Krishna debate, our questions can be broken down into those resting more on issues of integrity and those more on issues of consequences.

We believe that the duty of finance professionals is to take ethical responsibility for actions they are involved with or observe. They cannot devolve that responsibility to the company or its lawyers, managers or advisers. We also believe that a duty of financial professionals is not to engage in contrivances that put their business partners at a disadvantage. This resonates with the other age-old principle of not engaging in activity that would cause a breakdown of society if others were to do so as well. In the history of many countries, there were occasions when one business rival has facilitated the intimidation of another, forcing the rival to sell his business in a hurry at a knock-down price. This may sound like the actions of the robber barons of 19th-century America, but it is alleged that some short sellers follow the same route today by applying downward pressure on a firm's stock to a point where bankers' covenants are breached and the company's assets must be sold in a fire-sale or something similar. We elaborate a little more on short-selling in chapter 5 on investing and speculating.

On the issue of consequences, we believe that financial professionals should avoid all conflicts of interest that will potentially have a bearing on their final actions. This is easier said than done, especially in specialty areas of finance or small markets, so at least all potential conflicts should be disclosed. (Transparency is often touted as a way of improving the efficiency of markets but it may have more bearing on the ethics of markets and in turn their eventual inclusiveness.) We also believe, and we recognise that this is the most open ended of our ethical concerns, that finance professionals should consider whether they are causing harm to those not directly connected with the trade – stakeholders – and whether they have fully investigated ways of mitigating any consequential harm. In Benthamite terms, it is sometimes in the best interests of the many, that a dam is built that displaces the few. But there are many ways in which the harm caused to the few can be mitigated.

We hope to have shown through this book how these questions would have helped finance and business professionals to have better defined and reflected upon the ethical dilemmas they face.

➤ QUESTIONS SUMMARY

1. Am I devolving ethical responsibility to others?

2. Have I contrived a situation, or been party to a contrivance, which puts business partners to a transaction I am involved in, at a disadvantage to myself or the partners?

3. Are there disguised conflicts of interest in the transaction?

4. Have I considered the impact of a transaction I am financing, on the environment and the wider community, and how any harmful impact can be mitigated?

NOTES:

1 David Freud, *Freud in the City*, (Bene Factum Ltd, May 2006).

2 See "Adam Smith" by Lewis H. Ulman in *Eighteenth-Century British and American Rhetorics and Rhetoricians: Critical Studies and Sources*, ed. Michael G. Moran (Westport, Connecticut, 1994) 207 – 18.

3 See Hume's Moral Theory by Robert Shaver, *History of Philosophy Quarterly*, 12:3 (1995) 317 – 32.

INDEX

Plain English Business Titles

To order further copies call (+44) 020 7938 1975
or go to www.allyouneedtoknowguides.com